MAFIA AND OUTLAW STORIES
FROM ITALIAN LIFE AND LITERATURE

The first work of its kind in English, *Mafia and Outlaw Stories from Italian Life and Literature* is a selection of readings by noted Italian writers on the subject of the Mafia. Featuring short stories by important writers such as Giovanni Verga, Grazia Deledda, Anna Maria Ortese, Livia De Stefani, and Silvana La Spina, the collection also includes testimonies by famous witnesses Maria Saladino, Felicia Impastato, Letizia Battaglia, and Rita Atria, who provide personal, often terrifying, accounts of their experiences with the Mafia.

The stories, dating from the 1880s to the 1990s, offer a sampling of the diverse ways that Italians, as writers and citizens bearing witness, have represented the Mafia and crime in various historical contexts. While addressing the important values, myths, and images associated with the Mafia, the stories examine the many spheres of Mafia activity and the organization's influence on business, politics, the church, family life, Sicilian culture, and Italian society as a whole. Robin Pickering-Iazzi's thoughtful and engaging introduction charts key periods in the history of Italy and the Mafia, and profiles each of the authors in the collection, noting their major works in Italian as well as those available in English.

Mafia and Outlaw Stories from Italian Life and Literature takes an original and intriguing approach to the subject of the Mafia, and offers unique insight into its historical impact on Italian society and culture.

(Toronto Italian Studies)

ROBIN PICKERING-IAZZI is a professor in the Department of French, Italian, and Comparative Literature at the University of Wisconsin–Milwaukee.

Mafia and Outlaw Stories from Italian Life and Literature

Translations and Introduction by
Robin Pickering-Iazzi

UNIVERSITY OF TORONTO PRESS
Toronto Buffalo London

© University of Toronto Press 2007
Toronto Buffalo London
Printed in the U.S.A.

Reprinted 2008, 2011, 2013

ISBN 978-0-8020-9834-4 (cloth)
ISBN 978-0-8020-9561-9 (paper)

Printed on acid-free paper

Toronto Italian Studies

Library and Archives Canada Cataloguing in Publication

Mafia and outlaw stories from Italian life and literature / translations and
introduction by Robin Pickering-Iazzi.

(Toronto Italian Studies)
Includes bibliographical references.
ISBN 978-0-8020-9834-4 (bound) ISBN 978-0-8020-9561-9 (pbk.)

1. Mafia in literature. 2. Outlaws in literature. 3. Mafia – Italy – History.
4. Women and the mafia – Italy. 5. Italian fiction – 20th century –
Translations into English. 6. Italian fiction – 19th century – Translations
into English. 7. Women – Italy – Biography. 8. Crime in popular culture
– Italy. I. Pickering-Iazzi, Robin II. Series.

PQ4250.E5M33 2007   853'.910803556   C2007-905811-6

University of Toronto Press acknowledges the financial assistance to its
publishing program of the Canada Council for the Arts and the Ontario Arts
Council.

University of Toronto Press acknowledges the financial support for its
publishing activities of the Government of Canada through the Book
Publishing Industry Development Program (BPIDP).

Contents

Acknowledgments

Several friends, colleagues, and authors have contributed to the making of this book in uniquely enriching ways. I owe great thanks to Paolo Iazzi for his spirited reading and discussion of all the stories gathered here. Giovanna Miceli Jeffries deserves special mention for drawing my attention to the women's testimonies in *Le Siciliane*. I have deep appreciation for the various kinds of support for the project lent by fellow scholars Fabian Alfie, Salvatore Bancheri, Cinzia Blum, Norma Bouchard, Gary P. Cestaro, Valerio Ferme, Stephanie Jed, Geoffrey R. Skoll, Giovanna Summerfield, and William Van Watson. Dr. Nadia Furnari generously gave advice about Rita Atria's writings. I am grateful for the continued support of my research offered by the College of Letters and Science at the University of Wisconsin–Milwaukee. At the University of Toronto Press, Ron Schoeffel's expertise as editor and enthusiastic commitment to this book and to what it aspires to do have been extraordinary. Likewise, the stories have benefited from John St James's sharp eye and talent as a copy-editor. I also wish to thank the students who have read earlier versions of these materials, and eagerly shared their ideas on the complex historical, social, political, and moral issues that these stories and their telling raise.

I am indebted to the contributions of the following Italian authors and publishers, who generously gave permission for my English translations to be published here. I thank Silvana La Spina for 'La Truvatura' (1993); Flaccovio Editore for the excerpts from Luigi Natoli's *I Beati Paoli* (Palermo: Flaccovio, 1996); La Luna soc. coop. A r.l. for chapters from Amelia Crisantino's *Cercando Palermo* (Palermo: La Luna, 1990); Coppola Editore for the testimonies by Maria Saladino, Felicia

Impastato, and Letizia Battaglia, published in *Le Siciliane. Quindici storie vere* (Trapani: Coppola Editore, 1998); Sellerio for excerpts from Maria Occhipinti's *Il carrubo e altri racconti* (Palermo: Sellerio, 1993); and Adelphi Edizioni for 'Montelepre' by Anna Maria Ortese.

Every effort has been made to trace and contact copyright holders. The author would appreciate hearing from any copyright holders not here acknowledged.

MAFIA AND OUTLAW STORIES
FROM ITALIAN LIFE AND LITERATURE

Introduction: Not the Sopranos ... Viewing the Mafia and Outlaws through Italian Eyes

It's so funny because it's so real ... The only difference between Tony Soprano and me is that he's a mob boss.

Charles Albrecht, *New York Times*, 2000

After a number of such stories, the scent of orange and lemon blossoms starts to smell of corpses.

Leopoldo Franchetti, 1876

Since the publication of Mario Puzo's explosive best-seller *The Godfather* in 1969, a string of American novels, feature films, and television series have claimed to take us inside the minds, hearts, and 'families' of Mafia bosses. The significance and appeal of such stories among mass audiences in the United States have not escaped commentators, who underscore just how embedded the figure of the Mafia mobster is in the fabric of American popular culture. More to the point, in the wake of the acclaim garnered by the HBO hit series *The Sopranos*, Caryn James suggests that 'feeling inside a Mafia family has become a cultural touchstone.'[1] If so, this sense of being privy to insider information may lead viewers and readers to think that by now they have witnessed all there is to know about the so-called secret society of Cosa Nostra (Our Thing).

In fact, the features of the 'made men' and the plotting of their family exploits, trials, and tribulations clearly vary over the years, in vein with the changes in American society, culture, and target audiences. While investigating this field of inquiry in *Hollywood Italians*, Peter Bondanella insightfully charts the richly variegated, complex cast of Italian wise guys in the gangster-film genre, comedy, and television series produced from the silent era to the postmodern 'Sopranos.' Furthermore, books like Lynda Milito's autobiographical *Mafia Wife* reveal secrets of 'family life' that dash seductive images of the mafioso. Notwithstanding this diversity, the ways many Mafia stories are told on screen and off tend to appeal to American audiences' sympathies, in part by virtue of the insistent justification of the characters' criminal acts.[2] To be sure, such appeals offer important evidence about engaging desires, fears, fantasies, and values in the constantly changing landscape of American society. But they also run risks. Viewing mafiosi exclusively through the lens of American novels and films contributes to the tendency to take popular images of the Mafia and the criminal association that bears the same name and operates in Italian territory for one and the same thing. Furthermore, it encourages the inclination to collapse crucial distinctions between images of the Mafia as produced by the American cultural imagination and the various perceptions and meanings of it in Italian culture.[3]

This collection features stories from life and literature in Italy that make it possible for readers to discover, appreciate, and think about the variety of different ways in which Italian authors and witnesses have spoken about the Mafia as well as related figures or myths bearing upon it. Some readers may already be familiar with Leonardo Sciascia's novels *The Day of the Owl* and *To Each His Own*, which earned him enduring regard in the 1960s as the authority on literature, the Mafia, and Sicilian culture. More recently, such novels as *The Shape of Water* (2002) and *The Terra-cotta Dog* (2002) have introduced the American public to Andrea Camilleri's Montalbano mysteries, a virtual obsession among many Italians. Yet, as we see here, Italy has a long-standing, mercurial tradition of fiction and non-fiction writings that scrutinizes the Mafia from distinct intellectual and creative angles of vision. Indeed, the short stories and excerpts from novels selected for this collection represent works by some of Italy's most talented, award-winning storytellers. They range from Giovanni Verga, renowned for transporting readers into the lives of Sicilian peasants and townspeople, to the Nobel Prize–winner Grazia Deledda, whose enthralling outlaw tales expose forbidden passions, deeds, and dreams. Similarly, nearly a century after its original publication, Luigi Natoli's gripping saga of the secret Blessed Paulists sect continues to delight readers, many of whom retell their exploits from memory. The recipients of several literary prizes, Silvana La Spina and Amelia

Crisantino may also surprise if not shock us with their stories, which strip away the mythic guise of the Mafia's benevolent power. In the second section of the volume, testimonies provided by women of diverse generations who have witnessed first-hand the violent realities produced by the Mafia in their families and communities make an immeasurable contribution to our understanding of the various *cosche* (Mafia clans or families) and how they relate to the history of the Mafia's enterprises in business, society, politics, and culture.[4] Maria Saladino, Rita Atria, and Felicia Impastato lived in biological families adhering to Mafia culture, as determined by the mafiosi heading them. Letizia Battaglia has earned international fame for her photography documenting the infamous Mafia wars in Palermo, as well as the infinite facets of Sicilian life and culture. Each of these women has made remarkable achievements in the fight to defeat the Mafia.

Spanning over a century, the selections of fiction and non-fiction here offer a sampling of the diversified ways that Italians, as writers and citizens bearing witness, have represented the Mafia and related topics in various historical contexts, dating back to the 1800s. Most contemporary scholars locate the beginnings of the Mafia in the founding of the modern Italian nation (1860) and the development of agrarian capitalism, though certain values and practices that come to be associated with the Mafia through its own acts of appropriation are evident well before then.[5] For example, a pronounced sense of honour, individual autonomy, and *omertà*, a code of silence in the face of any state authority, are prominent features of Sicilian mores well before the 1800s. Likewise, scholars have traced the existence of such loosely associated, secret criminal societies as the *Stuppaghieri*, operating in the area of Monreale, and the *Fratuzzi*, controlling territory around Bagheria, back to the early nineteenth century. However, the earliest recorded references to the Mafia as criminal association appear in the 1860s, initiating the varied tradition of discourses to which the stories featured here contribute. In view of the sobering issues these authors put under scrutiny, it may be surprising that the first work in Italian literary history to portray the Mafia is a two-act comedy, written in Sicilian dialect by Gaspare Mosca and titled *I mafiusi di la Vicaria* (The mafiosi of the Vicaria). Set in the imposing Palermo Ucciardone prison in the year 1854, the play was first staged in 1862 by a Palermo theatre troupe. It met with resounding success and was taken on the road to theatres in Rome, Turin, and Milan, thus putting into farcical public view the inside story of a Mafia boss and underlings, their nefarious dealings, and particular jargon.[6] With more grievous implications and consequences, Prefect Marchese Filippo Gualtiero authored the first state document employing the term Mafia, alerting the Italian government to the rule of criminality creating dangerous conditions in Sicily in 1865, and calling for the deployment of troops.

Yet more pertinent here are the writings by the intellectuals Pasquale Villari and Leopoldo Franchetti, owing to their formative influences on images of the Mafia and debates about its causes, agents, and effects on Sicily and the Italian nation.[7] In March 1875 Villari first published analyses of the camorra, brigandage, and the Mafia in the form of three letters to the editor of the publication *Opinione* (Opinion), soon united with other articles in his famous *Le lettere meridionali* (Southern letters, 1878). Observing that the social strata of *gabelloti* (leaseholders), middlemen hired by absentee estate owners to lease out the land, and field guards represent the primary source of mafiosi, he describes the Mafia's virulent power to generate profit and violence, declaring, 'The Mafia makes money, takes its own revenge, kills, and even produces popular uprisings' (88). In similar fashion, Franchetti dispels any lingering illusions we may have of an 'old Mafia' operating as a benign system of mutual aid for the downtrodden. Based upon his on-site investigation of Sicily in 1876, he defines the Mafia as 'an industry of crime and violence.' (See John Dickie, *Cosa Nostra*, 50.)

The terms and definitions composed by Villari and Franchetti form one of the prominent veins of thought concerning the Mafia in Sicily, a controversial topic in the late 1800s, which inspired numerous studies in economics, sociology, and political science, as well as articles in newspapers and popular magazines. In this context, Verga's suspenseful short story 'The Gold Key' (1884) is especially thought-provoking. Here, though the armed field guard Surfareddu is never referred to explicitly as a mafioso, he is clearly encoded as such by the author's depiction of him as an agent of violence for hire to protect estate owners' property, the code by which he lives, and other signs. Through developments in plot and character, the author subtly delineates the roles he plays, directly or peripherally, in the collusive relations of power between landowners, representatives of the Catholic Church, and agents of the law. Verga also raises questions about justice both before and after the Unification of Italy in 1860.

Though published just one year after Verga's tale, 'An Episode of Brigandage' by Carolina Invernizio offers many significant points of contrast. Created from the perspective of a woman author of northern Italy, the story within a story gives us a unique view of brigandage, a popular theme in literature by Sicilian authors, which has profound implications for considering images of the Mafia in the social and cultural imagination.[8] Brigandage is the name the Italian state applied to what were predominantly peasant rebellions against the oppressive conditions of poverty levied by landlords in the southern provinces near Naples and in Sicily. Thus, political features historically distinguish brigandage, making it distinct from the Mafia.[9] In the sphere of cultural production, however, the Mafia enlists for its own service legendary aspects of the brigands as rebels defending the weak against a cruel, unjust society. The creative incorporation of such popular cultural myths into the ideology of the Mafia serves several functions. As Salvatore Lupo tells us, it provides rules that 'guarantee the organization's survival, cohesion, and capacity to find consensus as well as to inspire terror both on the inside and out.'[10] Invernizio's detailed, vivid descriptions of the brigands haunting the Edenic outlands in the provinces of Naples enable readers to pose intriguing questions concerning how the ideals, actions, and notion of justice she attributes to them may relate to those ascribed to Mafia characters in the stories by Verga, Nuccio, or La Spina, for example.

Luigi Natoli's serialized novel *I Beati Paoli* (The Blessed Paulists, 1909–10) is perhaps the most important literary work implicated in the mythic construction of rebel outlaw heroes secretly united to thwart an unjust system and execute justice for the powerless, of which the Mafia partakes. Jane C. Schneider and Peter T. Schneider (1994) offer evidence of the associations made between this literary text and Mafia culture in everyday life. As they recall, during their 1969 stay in a Sicilian town a local mafioso advised them that if they really wanted to understand the spirit of the Mafia they should read *I Beati Paoli*.[11] Contrary to such claims of parentage with the idealized image of the Blessed Paulists, there are no historical ties between the Sicilian Mafia and the secret sect. Instead, according to the multivolume diaries penned by the Marquis Villabianca in the late 1700s, the Blessed Paulists were a secret society of vindicators, whose origins purportedly reached back to the 1100s. As the excerpts from Natoli's popular historical novel illustrate, he is a masterful storyteller, whose riveting tale of murder, stolen birthright, torture, and vindication may engage readers on many levels. As he takes us through the twists and turns of Palermo streets and the subterranean city, he devotes meticulous attention to historical details shaping the geographic, social, political, and cultural landscape, conjuring life in the 1700s before our very eyes. At the same time, the story may appeal to common fantasies for the way he reveals the secret beliefs, rituals, and deeds of the sect, whose members right the wrongs suffered by the powerless, bringing down swift, unerring justice on the heads of the powerful who abuse their station in life.

Palermo also figures prominently in Giuseppe Ernesto Nuccio's short story 'Testagrossa Agrees' (1911). This author, however, depicts the markets and neighbourhoods of early-twentieth-century Palermo through the experiences of a homeless child. Renowned for his realistic portrayals of the dire conditions of urban poverty contributing to social problems, here Nuccio unites strains of humour, suspense, and tragedy as he draws us into a day in the life of Testagrossa, a most memorable character. The dramatic narration of the adventures encountered by this young boy, one of the countless children left to fend for themselves on the streets, describes his adversities, pain, and pleasures, while highlighting the differences between good and evil, the laws ruling the state and street, and the relations between poverty and crime. His struggle to negotiate these conflicting forces assumes tragically epic dimensions, mirrored by the story of chivalrous kings and knights performed by marionettes at the *Opera dei pupi*, the popular puppet theatre. This story is also remarkable for its critical perspective on the subject of the Mafia and children, a topical problem addressed in numerous works of Italian literature, film, and research. This trend is exemplified by Maria Rosa Cutrufelli's novel *Canto al deserto* (Singing to the desert, 1994) and Franco Occhiogrosso's edited volume of articles *Ragazzi della mafia* (Children of the Mafia, 1993). As an antecedent, Nuccio's story explodes the common notion that the Mafia does not prey upon or harm children, thus offering interesting points of comparison with the fictional tale by La Spina and the life stories told by Livia De Stefani, Saladino, and Impastato.

The historical frame of Italian Fascism and its antimafia front bears upon the selections by Grazia Deledda, Maria Occhipinti, and Livia De Stefani, which feature various types of outlaw figures – the hired killer, the member of the *Mano nera* (Black Hand), and the rural Mafia boss. In May 1924, nearly two years after becoming prime minister of Italy, Benito Mussolini made a trip to Sicily for a series of speeches that signalled the impending battle he would wage against the Mafia. Before the audience in Agrigento, he proclaimed he 'could not tolerate a few hundred criminals holding down a population as magnificent as yours.'[12] Indeed, for several reasons, including ideology, the changing political system, and the law-abiding public image of Italy Mussolini endeavoured to project, the Fascist state would target what has been called the Mafia state. From an ideological standpoint, the Fascist regime sought the complete loyalty and obedience of its citizens, members of the nation as 'family' headed by Mussolini.[13] Thus, even legitimate associations that might divide loyalties or challenge Fascist authority were outlawed. Furthermore, as Servadio notes, once Mussolini abolished elections in 1925, as one of several measures to consolidate the Fascist dictatorship, he had no need for the votes produced and sold by the Mafia, since the 1870s, to political figures and parties best serving its interests. That same year, Mussolini launched the antimafia campaign, designed and executed by Cesare Mori, the prefect of Palermo. Significantly, a new law was instituted the following year, stipulating that citizens could denounce anyone 'described by vox publica as bosses, partners or sympathizers of associations which have a criminal character or are in any way dangerous to the community.'[14] In such cases, the individual could be arrested and jailed, or sent into forced residence, with no trial. Just two years later Mori declared that the Mafia had been eradicated. However, the effectiveness of the violent, repressive measures utilized by Mori is not so clear.[15] Some people made use of the 1926 law to settle personal scores or to put leftist leaders out of circulation. And though hundreds of mafiosi were arrested, they tended to belong to the lower ranks. In fact, some historians argue that it was not uncommon for Mafia bosses to become prominent figures in the Fascist party.

The excerpts from De Stefani's autobiography *La mafia alle mie spalle* (The Mafia at my back, 1991) reveal extraordinary insights about the rural Mafia during Fascism and in the postwar years.[16] Born and raised in an aristocratic family that resided in Palermo, in 1930 she inherited the large ex-feudal estate of Virzì, located in the interior of Sicily near Alcamo. As the autobiographer recalls the impressions, experiences, and events linked to her attempts to actively manage the estate business, she produces vivid evidence of the weapons employed by the mafiosi in order to exert full power over the people, land, and affairs that fall within the territory they rule. She documents as well her face-to-face meeting with the famed Mafia boss Vincenzo Rimi and his son Filippo, which, she speculates, may be the only time a woman negotiated with a boss in the history of the traditional Mafia of western Sicily. De Stefani's life story is also unique for the way it inscribes the particular perspective of a woman estate owner in the descriptions of the peasant workers in her employ, and how they are situated vulnerably in the power relations shaping their lives and livelihoods.

Writing from different social positions and geographical locations, both De Stefani and Maria Occhipinti bring to light different dimensions of the crucial subject of the Mafia and its relation to the peasant class. Although reasons vary according to territory and socio-historical factors, as most historians agree, since the 1800s the Mafia has levelled its fiercest tools of oppression at the peasants, often with the aim of increasing its power through the alignment with wealthy property owners and political representatives of the Italian state. Furthermore, from the 1800s into the post–Second World War period, the efforts that members of the peasant class undertook to agitate for agrarian reforms posed challenges to the established system of power, and thus the Mafia. In fact, Umberto Santino credits the formation of the *Fasci siciliani* (Sicilian leagues), organized by peasants and leftist activists in the 1890s, with being the first organized battle against the Mafia.[17] In the case of the Sicilian leagues, which is hardly an exception, Mafia and government forces put down the peasant acts of militancy. Thus, it is not surprising if De Stefani's recollections of incidents bearing signs of the Mafia that befall peasant workers in the area have no hint of benevolence. On the contrary, the acts of intimidation and coercion threatening De Stefani as the owner of Virzì have potentially disastrous implications for the sharecroppers and labourers. Elaborating the subject of the lower classes more fully, Occhipinti's fictional tale, drawn from the story 'The Carob Tree,' focuses exclusively on the beliefs, traditions, and occupations that go into the making of life in a peasant community some time during the years of Fascism. In terms verging on the idyllic, the narrator describes what binds the neighbours together – their poverty, the roles of gender and generation structuring the family, the ethics of work and honesty, and even forms of popular entertainment. With the arrival of an Italian family repatriated from America, whose father is rumoured to be a member of the Black Hand, the author richly portrays the attitudes and behaviours demonstrated towards the newcomers and what the male head of household comes to represent in relation to social mores.[18] Occhipinti's images of the criminal and the thoughts that he elicits among the peasants offer interesting points of contrast and comparison with more recent representations of the Black Hand in Melania G. Mazzucco's *Vita. A Novel* (2005) and Francis Ford Coppola's well-known *Godfather II* (1974).

Published during the Fascist dictatorship on the cultural page of the nationally distributed newspaper *Corriere della sera* (22 February 1928), Deledda's short story 'The Hired Killer' speaks not about the Mafia or an affiliated member of a criminal association. As indicated by the title, the author creates a thought-provoking profile of a hired killer, a familiar figure in literature about the Mafia (Sciascia's *To Each His Own*, for instance), and in the history of the *cosche*. Indeed, at various historical junctures, the criminal association has made use of brigands, bandits, and mercenary killers, a point raised in Rita Atria's diary entries. While Deledda unfolds the tale of the protagonist's fortunes living inside and outside the laws regulating civil society, her imaginings on what goes into the making of a criminal engage with themes developed in several stories, especially in *The Blessed Paulists* and 'Testagrossa Agrees.' She invites us to think about the relations between the institution of the law delivering 'justice' and popular notions of justice; the reasons that drive essentially honest citizens to become outlaws; and the implications of taking the 'law' into one's own hands, becoming judge and executioner.

Revisiting the tumultuous landscape of postwar Italy, marked by a resurgence of banditry with links to the Mafia and the separatist movement, Anna Maria Ortese's 'Montelepre' beckons readers on a journey through land and time to the birthplace of Salvatore Giuliano.[19] Among the most famous, controversial figures in Italian history, Giuliano turned bandit in 1943 after killing a carabiniere who had caught him with a bag of black-market grain. For some seven years, Giuliano and his band committed an unbroken string of armed robberies and kidnappings and trafficked in the black market, with profits going primarily towards funding the separatist movement, which he had joined in 1945. For some, such exploits lent a romantic aura to the bandit, whose dark, brooding features were captured on the front pages of newspapers and the covers of such magazines as *Time*. At the same time, Giuliano and his band perpetrated violent attacks on the state, ambushing and killing carabinieri, and on members of the Communist and Socialist parties. Two of their most infamous assaults remain deeply inscribed in Italian cultural memory. The first is the 1947 Massacre at Portella della ginestra, in which Giuliano's band opened machine-gun fire on peasant women, men, and children gathered to celebrate May Day, killing eight of them and wounding thirty-three. Then, in August 1949, the band attacked the barracks at Bellolampo, leaving seven carabinieri dead and eleven wounded. Such heinous violence might suggest Giuliano would be viewed as purely criminal. But ideas about the bandit, his death, and what he symbolized have remained equivocal since he died. Once Giuliano lost his usefulness for the Mafia, he lost their protection too, and he was found murdered on 14 July 1950, the details of his death buried beneath a cover-up involving, it seems, members of the government, the carabinieri, and the Mafia. In the aftermath, he became a symbol of sharply divided ideas and feelings. For some he was a heroic rebel of the people and a fallen martyr for the cause of Sicilian independence. Others saw him as a traitor to the peasants and their struggle, and a cold-blooded killer. It is precisely this sense of the equivocal that Ortese conjures and attempts to penetrate in 1955, as she and a fellow traveller make their way from Palermo to Bellolampo, and finally Montelepre. The voicing of the travellers' desires to undertake an adventure in romantic lands famed for banditry as well as the distancing of the territory through sensorial and animal imagery echo the tendency to exoticize Sicily, denying its participation in history, civilization, and the changes of modern life. Yet Ortese's impressionistic representation of the journey to Montelepre, a town awash in pink, green, and white, and her attempts to read the people's faces for what they may say about Giuliano form a unique, provocative document of the times.

Both La Spina's short story 'The *Truvatura*' (1992) and Amelia Crisantino's novel *Cercando Palermo* (1990), ricipient of the 1990 'Luna-Arcidonna' Award, exemplify aspects of the groundswell of antimafia cultural production in Italian literature, film, the visual arts, and daily life that began in the 1980s. As revelations from the Palermo maxi-trials grabbed headlines, informing the public about new developments in the prosecution of some four hundred suspected mafiosi, which was conducted by Judges Giovanni Falcone and Paolo Borsellino, thoughts about the Mafia, antimafia forces, the justice system, and the Italian state preoccupied many Italians, including intellectuals and artists working in various media.[20] Published in the marvellous collection entitled *Scirocco*, La Spina's tale exhibits unexpected affinities with Verga's 'The Gold Key.' In the first lines of the story, set in the rural Margherito district, the author drops readers into the mystery of a young boy who has been found murdered, evoking the surrounding countryside's sights, smells, and sounds. As we follow in the steps of the carabinieri investigating the tragic case, popular beliefs, legends, and folklore emerge as part of the particular place and the chorus of townspeople inhabiting it. La Spina subtly crafts a dark web of power relations, which we alone ultimately perceive.

In contrast, the excerpts from Crisantino's novel afford a look at the traces of the Mafia in postmodern Palermo. Here, the spaces of streets, markets, cafes, and apartment buildings differ markedly from those traversed by the Blessed Paulists or Testagrossa, for they materialize polyphonically, through the eyes and words of several different, unforgettable characters: the Turinese Armando Berti, who has just earned his PhD from the Oxford Institute of Economics and Sociology, and arrives to theorize Palermo in terms of a non-sense city; the carriage driver, a visionary philosopher whose tourist routes include what he has named the route of civil indignation, featuring sites where the Mafia has murdered prominent public figures committed to justice and the defeat of the criminal association. The excerpts featured here represent the voices and views of three other characters – Signora Olga, her husband Don Pino, and Ida Benelli. Each of these figures says something about the formation and fortunes of the mafioso, as well as his relationships with 'grey zoners,' a term indicating individuals who are not affiliated members of the Mafia, but may traffic in information or favours. These forms of complicity enable Mafia activities to flourish. Among the other particularly important elements of the chapters of *Cercando Palermo* appearing here are, for example, the way the narrative both challenges the notion that unlawful behaviour, and the south in general, are necessarily irrational and alludes to the potential relationship between the Allied occupation of Sicily and the Mafia.[21] Indeed, some scholars argue that the American and British forces played key roles in the reconstruction and legitimation of the Mafia power base, strategically situating it to expand operations in the black market, postwar reconstruction, and politics. Furthermore, with the character Ida Benelli, Crisantino calls our attention to the relations between women and the

Mafia's entrepreneurial criminal activities. Since the 1980s, when explosive newspaper headlines reported cases of Italian women working as drug mules, registering Mafia properties in their own names, and performing various services in the kidnapping industry, the roles women craft in both Mafia and antimafia associations have attracted increasing attention. In film, for example, the protagonist in Roberta Torre's *Angela* (2003) makes drug drops as nonchalantly as she delivers shoes to her legitimate clients, thus calling to mind Benelli's cool-headed calculations on crime for profit. In contrast, Marco Amenta's 1997 documentary *One Girl against the Mafia* gives voice to Rita Atria's courageous acts as a state's witness against the Mafia. To their credit, such authors as Renate Siebert and Liliana Madeo have gathered interviews, historical materials, and documents that provide invaluable information about the range of stands and actions women take in relation to Mafia and antimafia activities.

The testimonial writings appearing in this collection represent but a few of the voices from the 1950s to the 1990s who have broken the silence and spoken out against the Mafia and its crimes.[22] Drawing upon their diverse experiences of living in close private and public quarters with Mafia *cosche* battling over various territories, each of the speakers reveals her particular observations, thoughts, emotions, dreams, and strategies of antimafia intervention. For instance, Maria Saladino gives words to the feelings of shock, shame, and disillusionment produced by the crushing discovery that she is the daughter of a mafioso. Her testimony, like Rita Atria's, inscribes the brief gesture to somehow deny any association between the father's identity as mafioso and the vicious murders committed by the Mafia. However, she ultimately does not equivocate, stating that even the so-called 'old Mafia' was the Mafia nonetheless, and spread terror. It is significant that Saladino's testimony suggests that she rebuilds her identity, marshalling the Christian principles she holds true and her desire to eradicate violence and the Mafia. She commits her life and work to building youth centres that provide children with a safe place to stay, care, education, and job training. As she forcefully explains, such works threaten the Mafia, which seeks to keep the poor locked in poverty so the criminal association has a monopoly on potential aid, and thus influence.

The cases of Felicia Impastato and Rita Atria exhibit certain similarities, for the way both women come to experience and publicly represent biological families fatally divided between Mafia and anti-mafia beliefs, values, and practices. Felicia Impastato recalls how she was caught in the middle of violent conflicts that flared between her husband Luigi, associated with the powerful Mafia boss of Cinisi, Gaetano Badalamenti, and her son Giuseppe. Like Saladino, Giuseppe Impastato devoted his life to rescuing young people from the Mafia's sway in the 1960s and 1970s. He deployed various strategies, creating cultural centres, a radio station, newsletters, and demonstrations, in order to inform young people about the Mafia as an industry of crime producing poverty, drug addiction, and murder. On the night of 8 May 1978 members of the Mafia staged Giuseppe Impastato's murder to look like a suicide or a failed terrorist bombing. They placed his body over a bomb that they exploded on the railway tracks. Felicia Impastato's memories of those years, her son's life and death, and the various investigations into the murder and the Mafia have come to exemplify the possibility of lived transformations from adherence to Mafia codes and behaviours to the development of antimafia ethics and practices. Indeed, as Felicia Impastato declares in her revealing interview with Anna Puglisi and Umberto Santino, *La mafia in casa mia* (The Mafia in my home, 1987), after the murder of her son Giuseppe it was assumed that she would retreat into silence, as would be customary in her case, as a widow of a mafioso. Instead, she began speaking out to everyone who would listen, denouncing the Mafia.

In many ways, Rita Atria has become a powerful symbol of the fight for truth, justice, and the defeat of the Mafia. She was raised in a family structured by such Mafia codes of behaviour as vendetta and *omertà*. Yet after the murders of her father Vito and brother Nicola, who were both agents and victims of the Mafia, she followed the example of her sister-in-law, Piera Aiello, and became a collaborator with justice. The testimonial writings that she produced, which appear here, include passages from an autobiography she had begun to write, entries from the diary she kept, and the essay exam that she wrote on the assigned topic of the Mafia. They provide incredible insights on several problems. For example, Atria's commitment to justice and to providing crucial testimony for the prosecution of several mafiosi is beyond reproach. At the same time, the entries in her diary, where she confesses her innermost secrets and fears, suggest that the recreation of her identity, as a collaborator with justice, is hardly easy. On the contrary, her perceptions of self highlight fragmentation, confusion, and wounds, expressing the profound trauma and loss that may derive, in part, from divided beliefs, loyalties, and loves. Providing official testimony about her father's and brother's criminal activities, for example, clearly serves the cause of justice, yet also betrays the two people she loves most – her two stars, as she calls them. Nonetheless, she expresses the conviction that the Mafia can be defeated, calling upon everyone to defeat first the Mafia within. Furthermore, she voices hope, which depends upon young people being made aware of a different world, where the Mafia does not determine who you are and what you do.

Hope, the strength of women, and the engaged commitment to change are also prominent ideals driving the life, art, and testimony of Letizia Battaglia, a photographer of international renown. While sharing her particular notions of photography as socio-cultural practice, she brings to life her memories of the years when she worked as a photojournalist for the newspaper *L'Ora*, covering sites of atrocious Mafia murders that reportedly claimed the lives of some one thousand people, many of them civic leaders, from the late 1970s to the early1990s. Battaglia's photographs of Mafia crime scenes had key importance in the prosecution of suspected Mafia criminals, as well as in the antimafia movement. Yet her work is equally important for the way it captures visual images of joy, goodness, and richly unique features of Sicily and the individuals making a life there. Battaglia's descriptions of the various initiatives she has undertaken to re-appropriate sites languishing in Mafia hands and transform the city of Palermo enable a deeper appreciation of what is at stake and the myriad ways to work for change.

By making available a variety of fiction and non-fiction writings about the Mafia and the myths that have gone into the making of its name, this collection may serve as a point of departure for an archeological project of gathering and examining different Italian voices that, for well over a century, have spoken in diverse mediums, and continue to make themselves heard. As illustrated by the writings featured here, there is a far-reaching tradition of cultural critique scrutinizing the Mafia from different vantage points. In the process, authors and witnesses turn their keen eyes upon related issues in various spheres of living: social attitudes, customs, and conditions; gender, class, and generational relations; the institutions of state and church; the meanings and workings of justice, as well as the means to achieve it. These stories from Italian life and literature also enable us to study the ways in which the Mafia appropriates certain popular legends and myths to serve its purposes. They thus promote an appreciation of the distinctions between Mafia and Sicilian culture and, perhaps, make new views of American popular culture possible as well. Moreover, the authors' different ways of speaking about the Mafia also open discussions about ideals, values, practices, and dreams that have long been engaged in the transformation of Italian life and society.

NOTES

1 See Caryn James, 'Addicted to a Mob Family Potion,' collected with articles by Charles Albrecht and Stephen Holden, among others, in *The New York Times on the Sopranos*. Many cultural critics have examined the representations of the Mafia in American popular fiction and film. Most pertinent here are Chris Messenger, *The Godfather and American Culture*; Peter Bondanella, *Hollywood Italians*; and George De Stefano, 'Ungood Fellas.'
2 See Elena Brancati and Carlo Muscetta for this Italian perspective, which they present in *La letteratura sulla mafia* (Literature about the Mafia). It should also be noted that Italian cinema has produced films about the Mafia and the code of honour in the tradition of Italian comedy, which tends to include strains of social critique. Some examples include Pietro Germi's *Seduced and Abandoned* (1964) and Roberto Benigni's *Johnny Stecchino* (1991).
3 On a related note, George De Stefano makes the crucial point that there is a prominent tendency in the United States to conflate the Mafia with the regional culture of Sicily and Italian culture in general.
4 See Renate Siebert's ground-breaking work *Secrets of Life and Death*, in which she examines a complex variety of positions that Italian women adopt in relation to Mafia culture structuring familial relations, to the criminal association, and to the antimafia movement and initiatives. Revelations made by male members of the Italian Mafia who have turned state's evidence are available in Pino Arlacchi's *Men of Dishonor*, among other works.
5 See Jane C. Schneider and Peter T. Schneider, 'Mafia, Antimafia, and the Question of Sicilian Culture'; John Dickie, *Cosa Nostra*; Raimondo Catanzaro, *Il delitto come impresa* (Crime as Enterprise); and Umberto Santino,

'L'omicidio mafioso' (Mafia Murder). In addition to securing monopolies over every resource imaginable, from water rights to illegal slaughter-houses, in the 1800s members of the *cosche* created markets for violence and murder. See also Gaia Servadio's analysis of the *gabelloti* (leasehold-ers). Several studies examine the key roles played by mafiosi and bandits in the 1860 revolution led by Garibaldi in Sicily, which culminated in the Unification of Italy. With respect to values and beliefs that have a long-standing history in Sicily, and may be appropriated by the Mafia, see Ida Fazio's salient study 'The Family, Honour and Gender in Sicily: Models and New Research.'

6 The play was published in 1896. Interestingly, Giuseppe Rizzotto, another member of the theatre troupe, revised the play, adding a third act that identified the incognito character as Francesco Crispi.

7 See Nelson Moe's *The View from Vesuvius* for brilliant analyses of the writings by Villari and Franchetti. All quotations from Villari are from the edition *I mali dell'Italia* (Italy's Ills). Those from Franchetti appear in *Condizioni politiche e amministrative della Sicilia* (Political and Administrative Conditions of Sicily).

8 Among the examples are Vincenzo Linares, *Masnadiere siciliano* (Sicilian Highwayman, 1841) and Nino Savarese *Storia di un brigante* (Story of a Brigand, 1931), as noted by Massimo Onofri. Maria Rosa Cutrufelli's *La briganta* (1990, trans. *The Woman Outlaw*, 2004) combines extensive archival research on women brigands and literary invention, enriching the themes and problems represented in this body of writings.

9 During the first five years of Post-Unification Italy, some 116,000 troops were deployed to quash brigand uprisings, resulting in the killing of over 5000 men and women engaged in the rebellions. John Dickie provides an insightful analysis of brigandage and notions of national Italian identity in his 'Stereotypes of the Italian South 1860–1900.' Onofri examines literary representations of brigandage and their relations to Sicilianism.

10 Salvatore Lupo, *Storia della mafia* (Rome: Donzelli, 1993), 107–8.

11 See 'Mafia, Antimafia, and the Question of Sicilian Culture.' Servadio reports that during trial proceedings, some lawyers for Mafia defendants invoke what we could call the Blessed Paulist defence, claiming a similar identity and role in an unjust society.

12 Quoted in Servadio, *Mafioso*, 73. For a more comprehensive, meticulously researched historical analysis of Italian Fascism, the Mafia, and Sicily, see Christopher Duggan's *Fascism and the Mafia*.

13 It must be emphasized that as Italians negotiated the demands made by

the Fascist state, they adopted a full range of responses in their lives, work, and politics.

14 Quoted in Servadio, *Mafioso*, 75.

15 Servadio, Duggan, and Dickie all conduct examinations of the laws, policies, and tactics deployed in this campaign, and discuss its potential results.

16 De Stefani creates a fictional portrait of a rural mafioso in her novel *La vigna di uve nere* (1953), published in English translation five years later with the title *Black Grapes*. In an interview with Sandra Petrignani (in *Le signore della scrittura* [Writing Women], 1984), De Stefani comments on the significance of the novel, stating she was 'the first one in Italy to speak about the power of the mafioso as something that requires a particular kind of male character: violent, reserved, authoritarian, and protective, worshipping his own power and the submission of other people' (94).

17 See Umberto Santino, *Storia del movimento antimafia* (History of the Antimafia Movement). Such cycles of peasant agitation for land reform and acts of repression on the part of the Mafia and/or the Italian government continue well into the post–Second World War period.

18 Brancati and Muscetta indicate that in the United States in 1929, an alliance between the Black Hand and the Mafia was ratified, and the resultant association was called Cosa Nostra. For different perspectives on the Black Hand see Servadio and Dickie. Bondanella conducts a fascinating analysis of the Black Hand in American films dating back to the silent era.

19 Both Servadio and Dickie discuss the relationship between Salvatore Giuliano and the separatist movement, the Mafia, and prominent public figures of the time.

20 Several highly informative histories and commentaries on Falcone, Borsellino, the Maxi-trials, and their aftermath have been written. In English, see Alexander Stille's *Excellent Cadavers*. John Dickie also devotes substantial attention to these figures and events.

21 Drawing upon military and government documents of the time, Servadio argues that the Allied forces had a strong hand in placing mafiosi in powerful positions controlling civic order and goods, and even colluded with the Mafia in the black market. More recently, scholars have begun to challenge some of these claims. Salvatore Lupo conducts a convincing examination of this kind in 'The Allies and the Mafia.'

22 Among the forerunners is Francesca Serio, the mother of Salvatore Carnevale, the trade unionist working for agrarian reforms who was

killed by the Mafia in 1955. During court proceedings, she publicly named the individuals involved. Francesca Serio's experiences are represented in Carlo Levi's famous work *Le parole sono pietre* (Words Are Stones, 1955). Siebert's *Secrets of Life and Death* discusses the cases of other women who have taken the courageous step to speak out against the Mafia and its crimes.

The testimony of Rita Atria, written in 1991–2, is the only one whose dating is certain. Those of Saladino, Impastato, and Battaglia were republished by Coppola Editore in 1998, but are drawn from earlier, different versions, and the sources are not cited.

The Gold Key

GIOVANNI VERGA

In the parish priest's country house in Santa Margherita, they were reciting the holy rosary after dinner when they heard a gunshot in the night.

The priest turned pale, the rosary still in his hand, and the women made the sign of the cross, pricking up their ears, while the dogs in the courtyard barked furiously. Almost immediately another gunshot returning fire thundered through the glen below Rocca.

'Jesus and Mary! What on earth could it be?' blurted the servant girl in the kitchen doorway.

'Quiet everyone!' exclaimed the priest, white as his nightcap. 'Let me hear.'

He went over behind the window shutter. The dogs had quieted down, and outside you could hear the wind blowing through the glen. All of a sudden the barking started up again, louder than before, broken fitfully by the sound of a rock striking the door.

'Don't open it! Don't open it for anyone!' the priest yelled, running to get his carbine that hung over the head of his bed below the crucifix. His hands were trembling. Then in the midst of the din they heard someone outside the main entrance yell, 'Open up, Father! It's me, Surfareddu!' No sooner had the estate manager living on the ground floor finally gone out to quiet down the dogs and unbolt the main door than the field guard Surfareddu came in, his face grim and the shotgun still warm in his hand.

'What's wrong, Grippino? What happened?' the frightened priest asked.

'What's wrong, Your Lordship, is that while you are sleeping and resting, I'm risking life and limb guarding all your stuff,' answered Surfareddu.

And he told them what had happened, standing in the doorway and swaying back and forth in his usual way. He couldn't fall asleep because of the heat, and had gone to stand in the doorway of the hut for a moment, over there on the little terrace, when he heard a sound in the glen where the orchard was, a sound his ears alone knew, and Bellina's, a mangy mongrel of skin and bones that stuck by his heels. They were knocking down oranges and other fruit in the orchard. A rustling sound the wind doesn't make, then silent spells while they filled up their sacks. So he got the gun standing beside the hut door, that old flintlock shotgun with a long barrel and brass fittings that he had in his hand.

Talk about destiny! Because that was the last night he was supposed to stay at Santa Margherita. He had given his notice to the parish priest at Easter, both of them in complete agreement. And on the first of September he was supposed to go to his new boss's estate, the one in Vizzini. Just the day before he had turned in each and every thing to the priest. It was the last day in August, a pitch dark night without any stars. Bellina went ahead of him, her nose to the wind, silently, the way he had taught her. He walked along very slowly, picking his feet up high in the hay so you couldn't hear it rustle. Every ten steps the dog turned to see if he was following her. When they got to the glen he softly said to Bellina, 'Back!' He took cover behind a large walnut tree. Then he let out a bellow, 'Hey there! ...'

A bellow, God help us! – the priest was saying – that gave you goose-bumps when you heard it come from Surfareddu, a man who had committed more than one murder in his profession as field guard. 'Then,' replied Surfareddu, 'then they shot at me point-blank – boom! Luckily I fired back at the flash of the rifle shot. There were three of them, and I heard screaming. Go look in the orchard, because the man I got must still be there.'

'Oh! What've you done, you scoundrel!' exclaimed the priest, while the women screamed among themselves. 'Now the judge and the rotten lawmen are going to come, and you're leaving me in a mess!'

'This is the thanks I get, Your Lordship?' Surfareddu snapped. 'If they'd waited to steal from you after I'd left your service it was better for me too. I wouldn't have had this other quarrel with the law.'

'Get off to the Grilli's right now, and tell the estate manager I sent you. Then tomorrow you'll get what you need. But don't let anyone see you, for the love of God! Now that it's prickly pear season, people are all over the hills. Who knows how much this thing is going to cost me. It would've been better if you'd turned a blind eye.'

'Oh no, Father! As long as I'm in your service, Surfareddu won't suffer any dishonour of this sort! They knew that until August 31st I was the one taking care of your farm. So much the worse for them! I don't waste my gunpowder for sure!'

And off he went with his rifle over his shoulder and Bellina following behind while it was still dark. No one slept a wink that night in the country house of Santa Margherita, for fear of the thieves and the thought of that man lying on the ground there in the orchard. At daylight, when wayfarers started to appear on the path across the way, at Rocca the parish priest, armed to the teeth and with all the peasants following behind, ventured to go and see what had happened. The women were yelling, 'Don't go, Your Lordship!'

But just outside the courtyard, they ran into Luigino, who had slipped in among all the people, getting underfoot.

'Take this boy away,' yelled his uncle the priest.

'No! I want to go see too!' the boy screamed. Afterwards, for as long as he lived, the spectacle that he had seen right before his eyes when he was so little stuck in his mind.

He was just a few steps into the orchard, under an old, sick olive tree, lying on the ground, his nose the sooty colour of the dying. He had dragged himself on his hands and knees onto a heap of empty sacks, and stayed there the whole night. His companions had run away, taking the full sacks with them. There nearby was a stretch of dirt, gouged by fingernails and all black with blood.

'Ah! Your Reverence,' mumbled the dying man. 'They killed me over a couple of olives!'

The parish priest gave absolution. Then toward noon, the judge arrived with the lawmen and was bent on taking it out on the parish priest and tying him up like a scoundrel. Luckily all the peasants were there and the estate manager with his family as witnesses. Nevertheless, the judge vented his anger on that servant of God who was a sort of old-fashioned baron with his overbearing ways, and he had men like Surfareddu working for him as field guards, and had people killed over a couple of olives. He wanted the murderer handed over dead or alive, and the parish priest swore up and down that he didn't know anything about it. So much that just a bit more and the judge would declare him an accomplice and the one who gave the order, and have the rotten lawmen tie him up all the same. So they were yelling and coming and going under the orange trees in the orchard, while the doctor and the town registrar went about their tasks in front of the dead man laying on the empty sacks. Then they put the dining table in the shade of the orchard, because it was so hot, and the women coaxed the judge into eating a little something because it was getting late. The servant girl rolled up her sleeves: macaroni, tasty dishes of all sorts, and the women went out of their way so that the table wouldn't make a bad impression on that occasion. The judge licked his fingers. Then the registrar pulled the tablecloth back a bit from a corner and quickly drew up ten lines for the statement, with the witnesses' signatures and everything, while the judge had a cup of coffee made specially with the coffee machine, and the peasants watched from afar, half hidden among the orange trees. Finally, the parish priest went personally to get a bottle of aged Moscardello that would have made a dead man rise. Meanwhile, they had buried the other one as best they could under the old, sick olive tree. As he left, the judge accepted a bunch of flowers from the women, who had two beautiful baskets of chosen fruit put in the saddlebags on the registrar's mule. And the parish priest accompanied them all the way to the end of the farm's property.

The following day a District messenger came to say that the judge had lost his watch-key in the orchard, and they should look for it carefully because it certainly had to be there.

'Let me have two days' time, and we'll find it,' the parish priest had him reply. Right away he wrote to a friend in Caltagirone to have him buy a watch-key – a beautiful gold key that cost him two *onze*,[1] and he sent it to the judge, saying, 'Is this the watch-key that you lost, Judge?'

'This is it, yes, sir,' he replied. The trial smoothly went its way, so smoothly that 1860[2] suddenly came about, and Surfareddu returned to work as a field guard after Garibaldi was pardoned, until he got himself killed, struck with stones in a scuffle with some other field guards about a certain matter concerning grazing pastures. And the parish priest, whenever he would bring up the subject of all the things that happened that night and gave him so much to take care of, would say about the judge, back then, 'He was an honest man! Because instead of losing just the watch-key, he could have had me look for the watch and chain too.'

In the orchard, under the old tree where the olive thief is buried, grow cabbages as big as the heads of babes.

NOTES

1 The *onza* was a form of Sicilian currency, valued at 12.75 lire, a large sum
   in the mid-1800s.
2 Performing the first in the chain of actions to accomplish the Unification
   of Italy, Garibaldi and his thousand volunteers landed in Marsala in May
   of 1860, and launched a revolution against the ruling Bourbons, who ultimately abandoned Sicily. In October of the same year, following a
   plebiscite, the Kingdom of the Two Sicilies became part of the Kingdom
   of Italy.

An Episode of Brigandage

CAROLINA INVERNIZIO

One evening of late, a lively troupe of a few high-spirited women and vivacious young men was gathered in a villa. To break the monotony, they were chatting pleasantly among themselves, one saying this, another that. Suddenly a sprightly young woman jumped up to say:

'Signor Carlo (he was a young engineer, generally admired for his spirit and distinguished manners), come on, tell us one of your stories! Some adventure, for example, you had during your travels. I can't imagine you haven't had any. But be careful not to break into lofty flights and not to digress more than necessary. And above all, try not to exaggerate.'

'Thank you for the compliment, which is as much as to say don't concoct some silly story. Rest assured, I'll heed the advice. I shall simply tell you about what happened to me during my last trip in the Neapolitan provinces. Are you satisfied?'

'Yes, yes! But get on with it ...'

The young man smiled, and seeing how attentive and ready to listen to him everyone was, he began his story:

'Anyone who hasn't spent some time in the Neapolitan area can't imagine the unexpected radiance adorning nature there. The sun, when it rises and sets, bathes the lands with indescribable magnificence. Up above, you see the mountains in such a spectrum of deep red hues that even those with souls less poetic than mine would be carried away. A morning journey through these parts at the end of September has such attractions that its traces leave their mark on the soul for a long time. Since I was in Beneventano, I got the idea of taking an excursion up in the mountains, to admire the enchanting scenery that greets the eye everywhere you look. It's true that taking trips in the mountains was not very safe, and had kept travellers away from the area. But to tell the truth, I didn't believe in brigands. I had heard a lot of talk about them during my travels, but had never met up with one.

'On the other hand, I would have been very happy to know what a brigand might be, and I somehow felt that I would have experienced a certain satisfaction at being close to a person who was so dangerous. Therefore, I hired two mules and a guide. He was a strong young man of average height, but rather stocky in appearance, a real chatterbox, a poet should the occasion arise. So I expected to have good company. At first we came upon a lot of villas, rustic houses, the sort of rustic houses where herdsmen and shepherds usually live. But then the path became steep and rocky, worn into the bare sandstone. For as far as I could see in every direction, there wasn't a sign of a living creature.

'The further along we went, the more the scene changed appearance. I stopped for a moment on those cliffs, terrified by the grandiosity of the mountainous spectacle that appeared before me. On one side gaped the dark throat of a deep chasm, whose depths were impenetrable to the eye. But it looked to be bristling with intricate masses of thorns and brambles. On the other side, a thick forest stood behind a very sheer mountain, barren of trees or grass. Further off was a valley, with meadows, fields, country homes. Then the view stretched into the distance, the objects becoming smaller until everything finally disappeared in the horizon. In the meantime, we heard the sound of a distant country song, with a chorus of country girls singing along and the mountains echoing the words. A light breeze was gently blowing, invigorating our limbs. It heightened my imagination, and without my bidding I felt my soul transported to that sense of sweetness one experiences at the first smile of chaste love, at the throbbing that moves the first tender friendship. Our mules had little bells hanging from their necks, which made a tinkling sound, the only one that could be heard in those parts. We had gone about four miles when my guide got off his mule and carefully wrapped up its bells, doing likewise to the ones on my mule. In a low voice he said, "Here we have to be careful and stay absolutely quiet. A single word or a sound could alert the brigands. You see those woods, Signore? That's where they hide. No one would dare go through them. They go a little here and a little there, depending on which way the wind blows. Spirits are also in there with them, and at night, on those slopes, you see ghosts, monsters, skeletons, and odd lights."

'I was laughing heartily at his words when my guide suddenly exclaimed, "I think I hear the trampling of footsteps ... Don't you hear something, Signore?"

'I reigned in my mule and strained my ears. It was a rather faint sound in the trees. "It's the wind," I said.

'"No, no Signore, it's them. May the Virgin Mary and Saint Gennaro protect us!"

'We spurred our mounts' flanks, but in vain. The mules just trod along. While I kept silent and my guide cursed, the shots of firearms reached our ears and a few bullets whistled over our heads.

'"My God!" screamed my guide. He slid off his mule and took off at such a run down the other side of the mountain that I lost sight of him in a few minutes. Still shaken by surprise, I quickly regained my senses when I saw eight men armed to the hilt appear at my sides. Alone, unarmed, with no idea where I was, it would have been folly to try to defend myself. At first I thought they might just want to search me, and I was preparing myself to spare them such an inconvenience when one of them said to me:

'"Slow down! Slow down ... We want a lot more than your money bag. When a prize bird happens our way, we don't let it fly away so easily. Whether you want to or not, you have to come with us. If you resist, these will be enough to keep you quiet." Then half a dozen knives were levelled with the tip of their blades pointed right at me. But I fearlessly stood my ground, piercing my lips in such a look of disdain for death that the brigands, won over, slowly lowered their weapons and looked upon me more favorably, since courage is also necessary in crime.

'They made me get off the mule, and tied a rope around my waist. One of the brigands took the ends of the rope, and I was forced to walk in front of them. We went into a forest. I had all the time and leisure to contemplate the nature around me. The giant chestnut trees, oaks, and poplars towering above caught to wondrous effect the sun's rays, which tinged with an almost gloomy hue the plants in the forest, a very carefully chosen theatre for so many misdeeds. Huge masses of foliage, wild grasses, obstructed the deserted paths. It was, in short, quite a sight to behold, and filled my soul with a rush of emotion. At that moment, I felt the conviction of my own impotence. It was a new world meeting my eyes, but an inert world, full of silence, where everything inspired terror.

'Meanwhile, the brigands were talking and laughing among themselves. They had big, round, meaty limbs; olive-skinned, calm faces, toughened by the harsh weather; black, gleaming eyes; unkempt hair swaying to-and-fro above their shoulders, their wide foreheads buried beneath very broad-brimmed hats. They wore roomy jackets made of brown frustian, which revealed a glimpse of a black velvet jerkin with big gilded buttons. Their pants were also velvet, held up by a wide red band, from which two pistols hung. They wore leggings.

'We had reached a path that was so narrow we had to pass one at a time. Two men with brutal, ugly faces stood guard at the entrance. After the who-goes-there, we continued along the path, walking between deep purple rocks and cavernous ravines. The rustling of the dry twigs beneath our feet was the only sound breaking the deathly silence of those parts. Some time later, we entered a dense thicket. One of the brigands opened a door, carefully hidden among the plants. We went down just a few steps into a narrow, tortuous passage. At the end of it there was a large, poorly lit room, equipped with just a few pieces of furniture and paved in stone. We stopped here, and one of the brigands, the leader, untied me. He then put me through a sort of interrogation to find out who I was and where I came from. I answered frankly, in fact, with a certain arrogance. Afterwards, I was taken to a room nearby, lit by a weak light. As I walked across the room, I heard the man who had interrogated me say to the others, "He'll have to pay a hefty price for his ransom if he doesn't want to end up like the last ones we've had ..." At the sound of those words, I confess, I felt a chill run through my veins. Nonetheless, I didn't let my face betray a hint of emotion.

'When we went into the room, my guide exclaimed, "Here's another prisoner for you." I turned around to see whom he was talking to, and my eyes fell upon a woman so pretty that a slight expression of surprise escaped me. She was very young. The goodness of an ingenuous, gentle soul, virginal modesty, and maternal love were painted on her snow-white face. Calm and silent, she sat holding a lovely baby boy who did not even wake up with the din of the weapons and rough voices. I was watching that young mother, that smiling victim of love, and her lovely little child, with rosy cheeks and curly hair, when the leader of the brigands came into the room.

'"Gillo, my Gillo," said the woman, smiling. "So you're back?"

'"Yes, Carmela," the brigand replied, without a shadow of affection. "As you see, I brought a good catch with me. I'll leave him for you to watch over while we have something to eat."

'Turning to me, he said, "After we've finished our meal, you'll have yours. Meanwhile, we'll reckon accounts. But first I have to take care of a simple formality ..." He pulled out a long thin rope.

'"So is it necessary for you to tie me up?" I asked, taking a step back and leaning almost instinctively against the wall of the cave.

'"Extremely necessary. You might get it into your head to throw some punches. You're strong and brave."

'An ironic smile grazed my lips.

'"Don't worry," I replied. "I won't move from this spot."

'"And what token of faith will you give me so I could trust you?"

'"My promise."

'He said nothing.

'"I swear!" I repeated adamantly.

'"Now I've nothing left to fear," Gillo said. He left without even a glance at his wife or a word of affection.

'Carmela's eyes followed him anxiously, and she sadly bowed her head. I thought of how deeply the poor woman must suffer, bound forever to the man of crime, forced to share her food with him, and her bed, suffocating her leaping heart, the need to shed tears.

'I let out a sigh, which gave the woman a start. She passed her right hand over her forehead, pushed her black hair off her face. After taking a long look at me she got up, laid the child down gently on two chairs, opened a cupboard, and then brought out a bottle and a glass. She came close to me and in a quiet, touched voice she said, "Please have some of this strong drink. You must need some. It's all I can offer you."

'She insisted in such a charming manner that I couldn't refuse. Then there began between us one of those simple conversations that usually take place between a person in need and a benefactor, and reveal an entire life.

'Carmela loved that man, bound to him by destiny and because he was the father of her innocent little child. But at the same time, she was shocked and horrified at the sight of so many wicked deeds that were committed every day under her very eyes. They wanted her to stay close to the prisoners, and she aimed to be the guardian angel of the hapless. She had foiled the brigands' tricks, thwarted their plots many times. She had just turned twenty, the age of sweet illusions, hopes, and love, and was living there, buried away in that haven of crime. Her whole life was there now, and her future was there too. And yet, in the midst of that life full of sacrifices and privations, she silenced her own sorrows so that she could hear only those of others.

'Meanwhile, the brigands' cheers and drunken bursts of laughter could be heard from the nearby room. They were throwing the empty bottles, which made an unimaginable crash when they hit the ground.

'Carmela went on talking, now and then giving her son a look, a look that by itself revealed all the worry in the mother's heart. It had been a long time since the poor woman had felt the ineffable consolation of unburdening her tormented soul with someone who could accept her, sympathize with her, and give her compassion. She yielded to the impulses of a simple heart, one needing to emanate affection in words. We were both moved. Within me was pure, affectionate compassion; within her, the release of a flood long held back.

'A few moments of silence passed, then Carmela said, "Forgive me Signore, if I have been so bold ... but you seem so good. It's nearly impossible that someone might say a word of affection to me. My husband has no looks to relieve my loneliness, nor my son words. The prisoners they bring here to me are always in such a state of terror that they're horrified at the things I offer too."

'She was silent for a moment, then went on, "You're brave, Signore, and maybe that will avail to save you. Gillo is not a monster. He has a great soul, even in the midst of crimes. He abhors cowards, the weak ... and he loves and respects the valiant. Don't lose heart! I'll do what I can to save you, or at least to ease your captivity."

'In the middle of all the confusion and muffled talk that reigned in the room nearby, all of a sudden, we heard a voice yell, "To the lookout!"

'Gillo came into the room. His face had a brutal look of pride. He said to Carmela, "Our comrades at the look-out point have been attacked ... we're on our way to help them. But those soldiers, the damned bastards, will pay a dear price for our heads! Don't move from here! This hideout is safe."

'Turning to me, he exclaimed, "Stay put if you don't want to get acquainted with our blunderbusses!" Then he ran out.

'We were left alone. Carmela looked up at the heavens. She was thinking of me. "In all this turmoil, you're free to run," she said in a trembling voice, "they won't blame anyone."

'"But what about you?"

'"Don't worry! He won't dare touch me. Come with me!" She stopped a moment to gaze at her son, who was still sleeping. She was a mother. That was enough to understand what flood of emotions was suddenly welling in her soul. But recapturing at once a wonderful courage, she said, "Let's go! No one would want to take their rage out on an innocent little child."

'Since I was hesitating, she forcefully exclaimed, "I insist!" Then she gently added, "I beg you."

'Astonished and touched by her incredible steadfastness, I could only respond by squeezing the hand that had taken mine. Carmela opened a small door, which I had not seen before, and after a few steps down a passageway we were out in the open air. From the opposite direction we heard an exchange of shouts, shots, and curses that startled the courageous woman. In spite of it all, she herself insisted on being my guide through the unknown paths, and lead me down them to the edge of the woods. Then, without a word, she pointed the way to go.

'"May God bless you," I said, pressing her hand hard against my lips. "You can be sure that I will never forget you."

'Carmela seemed touched. "Pray for me!" she replied with a sad smile.

'"Will we see each other again?"

'She turned her eyes to the sky and replied, "Up there, where we are all equal."

'Bidding me one last farewell, she hurried away. My eyes followed her. The moon had risen rather high and penetrated the thick foliage. Its rays illuminated the worthy woman, whose steps were watched over by angels in that moment.

'An hour later I was safe ...'

The End

The Blessed Paulists

LUIGI NATOLI (WILLIAM GALT)

Part I, chapter XI

The Monte di Pietà clock had just struck midnight and the city was unusually alive with activity. That morning, October 10th, the thirty British and Genovese war vessels that were carrying Vittorio Amedeo,[1] his court, and retinue to the capital of the kingdom had arrived. They landed first at Arenella, where they received the archbishop, and shortly thereafter some noblemen and two members of the Senate. Then towards evening the ships cast anchor in the Molo Grande, and the king expressed his wish to go ashore the next day at about twenty-three hours Italian time.

A virtual army of artisans had spent the entire day feverishly attending to decorating the disembarkation bridge at Calla and the four arches in Piazza Villena. They were still busily at it now by the light of torches and candles, trying to finish up the work before daybreak. A coming and going of wagons and carts, the resounding sounds of hammers, yelling, and noisy racket amplified by the night spread through Cassaro and intensified at Quattro Canti, echoing through the entire city and beckoning the curious.

The idea of having a king of their own had infused their hands with the enthusiasm of their souls. There was patriotism in the fervour of those artisans, in the very curiosity of the citizens who, instead of going off to get some sleep, were staying at Quattro Canti or Calla to watch the people at work, as if encouraging them with their presence to get things done fast and well. The people who were sleeping that night had a light, sweetly anxious sleep. Those preparations for the solemn entrance and coronation were not the ones that took the most time and work. But they were enough to enliven and animate the city.

Everyone's attention was so drawn to the two city centres with the most work going on, and so many were walking about that even at that unusual hour no one was surprised to run into other people in the streets.

Two men cloaked unrecognizably in mantles drawn up around them left the Conceria quarter, crossed Strada Nuova, and slipped into Strada dei Candelai, but only after they had looked all around with the air of people who do not want to be followed. When they thought they had gone far enough so they could not be seen by all the new faces in the beautiful street, they left off walking like people just going about their own business and hastened their steps, like people who fear they will arrive somewhere late.

They turned towards Piazza Monte di Pietà and proceeded through Strada delle Lettighe, up to the Chiesa dei 'Canceddi,' or, rather, the Church of the Carters, commonly known by the name Santa Maruzza among the locals. There they stopped. One of the two men took his hands out from under his mantle, saying, 'Be patient. Let me blindfold you.'

The other man did not resist. The first one tied a scarf over his eyes and took him by the hand, adding, 'Come along. You'll be safe.'

They went along the side of the church, entered a dark, mysterious alley, and stopped after a few steps. 'We're here!' said the guide. He went up to a small, low door, worm-eaten and gashed, and scratched it lightly with his fingernail, like a cat. After a brief interval, another scratch replied from inside. Then the man made a faint whistle. The door opened without a sound. The guide took the blindfolded man by the hand and pulled him up close in the deep, dark space, saying, 'Come along. Mind, there's a step.' The door closed again behind them.

They went through a short passageway. At the end of it, another small door opened in the same mysterious way. They entered a little courtyard, with a crooked tree standing in the middle of it, blackened by the night. The pavement echoed under their steps in the night, as if it were hollow. 'Careful!' the man leading warned, 'Here we go down.'

Indeed, they went down some steps. The blindfolded man felt the air turn damp, and it smelled mouldy. The stairway, in fact, went down a passageway dug out of the tufa, which was incrusted here and there, making the ground slippery. A small oil lamp placed in a little niche carved in the wall shed just enough light for one to guess where the steps were. At the foot of the stairway they stopped. The guide said, 'Wait here a moment. Someone will come get you.'

He left the blindfolded man in some kind of room, and knocked five times on a door. A voice on the other side whispered some mysterious words, which the guide exchanged. The door opened and he entered a room lit by lanterns attached to the wall. Some voices greeted him.

'Good evening, Zi'[2] Rosario.'

The small shopkeeper's pockmarked face and lively little eyes appeared in the light of the lanterns. 'He's here,' he said. 'When you wish, Your Lordship ...'

At the end of the room there was a sort of altar made of stone, with a crucifix standing on it between two burning candles. At the foot of the cross was an open book. In front of the altar there was a small table at which three masked men, dressed in some sort of black robe, were sitting. Another six men, also wearing robes and masks, were sitting in high-backed chairs on each side of the room. Their eyes gleamed sinisterly beneath the masks.

Zi' Rosario went over to the wall, stuck his hands in a niche, and pulled out a bundle. A moment later, dressed in a robe and wearing a mask, he was no more recognizable than the others. Then the man who seemed to preside over the meeting made a sign. One of the six men stood up and left, and then returned almost immediately, leading the blindfolded man by his hand. 'Let him see the light,' ordered the leader.

The blindfold was removed and Andrea's astonished, agitated face appeared. The sudden passage from darkness to light prevented him from seeing the room clearly for a minute. Then little by little his eyes became accustomed to the light, and during the moment of silence that reigned in the room, he looked in amazement at the place where he stood, almost unable to bring himself to believe that in the heart of Palermo there could be such caverns, which, not uncommon in the outskirts of the city, the people attributed to the Saracens. The room was dug out of the tufa with a certain artistic criterion. It had a vaulted ceiling, and some niches carved in the walls. Near the altar there were traces of plaster, but the dampness had eaten it away. You could feel that grotto was located in the subsoil.

The leader asked him, 'Is your name Andrea Lo Bianco?'

'Yes, Your Lordship.'

'There are no Lords here. There are only brothers.'

'I beg your forgiveness.'

'Were you the servant of the late Duke of Motta?'

'Right up till the day he died at the hands of the Turks ...'

'Good. It has come to this venerable society's knowledge that you can furnish information about the current Duke of Motta ... Mind, solid information and documents are needed. Words alone won't satisfy us. We are involved in performing a work of justice and vindication, but we haven't been able to take a step because we ran into a closed door, which you can perhaps open.'

The leader was quiet for a minute, then began speaking again, in a solemn voice full of emotion:

'Andrea Lo Bianco, you have entered a place where no profane man has ever set foot. But this commits your life perhaps in a way you can't imagine. Are you certain you will keep your promises? If you aren't, state so now. Someone will take you away the same way you came, and you will be let free. We trust in your silence. But if you state you are certain, mind you, Andrea Lo Bianco, we will never again allow you to leave, and beside you, behind you, in the street, in church, in your very own home, there will always be the invisible and infallible vindicatory arm of our justice ...'

Andrea replied:

'I have faith in you. Have faith in me. You are here for justice, and I for vendetta. You saved me, and you are the masters of my life. I put all of my being at your service.'

'Good. Brothers, you may begin.'

The six men rose and encircled Andrea. There was a signal, and then all at the same time they pulled out long, sharp daggers from under the black robes covering them, and flashed the tips of the daggers before his eyes. Then two of them quickly grabbed Andrea, stripped his left arm, and carved a small cross on it with the tip of the dagger. The blood blossomed on his naked arm. Then one of the three men sitting at the small table stood up, took the book from the foot of the crucifix, and placed it on the table. He pulled a pen out of a small box and, after dipping it in the blood, handed it to Andrea.

'Andrea Lo Bianco,' said the leader, speaking again, 'this book contains the evangelical gospels and the letters of Saint Apostle Paul. Make the sign of the cross with your blood on this page, and swear to blindly obey whatever you are ordered to do. Swear it on the saint evangelists, on the Saint Apostle Paul, on your blood, which will be spilled drop by drop. Swear that you will keep the secret of what you will hear and see, and that neither torture nor temptations will wring even a sound from your lips. Swear that your body and your soul belong now and forever to this venerable society of the Blessed Paulists, in service of justice, in defence of the weak, against all forms of violence and domination committed by the government, the nobles, and the priests.

With a steady hand, Andrea drew a large cross at the foot of the page that the leader showed him, and said, 'I swear. And may this cross drawn with my blood mark my sentence if I fail to fulfil my obligation.'

'May God help you and may the Blessed Apostle Paul arm you with his zeal and give you his sword! Now, answer the questions. Were you in the service of Duke Don Emanuele?'

'Yes, Signore.'

'Until his death, did you say?'

'He died in my arms. But before he died he gave me a medal, so that I would place it around the neck of his sweet little son, whom he never saw. Once I returned to Palermo, after some ups and downs, I carried out the piteous task.'

The comrade sitting to the right of the president asked excitedly, 'And what about the medal?'

'It was a silver medal. It had a relic, a tiny fragment, mounted on one side, and the image of Saint Sebastian, the protector of the ancient Academy of Arms, engraved on the other. It hung on a small, silver chain ...'

'Ah! Good!' exclaimed the Blessed Paulist.

'Continue,' said the leader.

'I intended to watch over the little master, and had found a faithful companion in Maddalena. But I was sent away by Don Raimondo, and Maddalena was killed, maybe poisoned.'

'What makes you suppose that?'

'Don Raimondo tried to poison the duchess. He went with his trusted servant to get the poison at the home of a witch, who lived in S. Onofrio lane. She was called Peppa la Sarda. I heard what they said, standing behind the door. When they left, I burst into Peppa la Sarda's house and forced her to give me the antidote. For safety's sake, I gagged the witch and took her to my house. But all of my efforts were in vain. The duchess was surely murdered, and the son was murdered too. In order to hide the crime, Don Raimondo feigned that assassins had kidnapped them. He fastened a rope to the parapet of the balcony to simulate the kidnapping. Then he threw suspicions on me. I was arrested and thrown in prison. He's a murderer, Sirs, a murderer. He killed three innocent people in order to seize a patrimony that he's not entitled to.'

'Who's the servant?'

'I don't know if he still has him in his service. His name was Giuseppico. He was Majorcan, slender, dark-skinned, surly.'

'And what happened to Peppa la Sarda?'

'I don't know. The same night, when I went back home she wasn't there anymore. How'd she escape? I don't know. Where did she find a safe place to hide? We need to track her down. She supplied the poison two times, and one night she went to the palace to prepare it herself, and gave it to the mistress, thinking she was Maddalena. Oh, it's a sad, vile, wicked story! If Don Raimondo had the witch under his power, he would certainly have made her disappear. But if she's alive, she is a witness, in fact, a terrible accuser. She and Giuseppico. Poor Maddalena could have told a lot more ... but she's dead, the victim of her devotion to the mistress. So we must track down Peppa la Sarda and Giuseppico. They can't possibly be dead. Weeds never die. They must be holed up some place. Find them, force them to tell the truth. Then carry out justice. The souls of the victims, of Madam Aloisia, the little Don Emanuele, and Maddalena will bless you and finally have peace.'

Andrea's eyes were shining, while waves of emotion washed over his face, and hate and love ebbed and flowed in his trembling voice. A soft murmur followed, as if commenting upon his final words. The Blessed Paulist who had addressed the question about the medal to Andrea stood up then and exclaimed with feeling, 'God is just! God is great! God sent this man to us so that justice may be full and complete. *Dominus pupillum suscipiet, et vias peccatorum disperdet.*'

Andrea did not understand the Latin words, but he guessed they must have referred to the things he had told them. From the emphasis placed on the words, he gathered that there was something he did not know, but that had to be terrible. The Blessed Paulist who had spoken continued, 'I have some news that may be of interest, to which, indeed, I draw this venerable court's attention. The Duke of Motta has welcomed a guest in his home, a young man called Blasco da Castiglione, or at least he is going by that name. This young man was recommended to him by a friar at the friary of the Chiovari, Father Bonaventura da Licodia. He's a valiant young man, and it seems that the duke keeps him by his side for protection. My information says that he is truly a force to be feared.'

'It's true,' another man said. 'He gave a thrashing to those scoundrel police agents. He was lodging at the inn of the Messinese.'

Then the leader said, 'We need to find out who he is and where he comes from.' Turning to Andrea, he added, 'Stay on the ready for your orders, which will be communicated by the brother who led you here. In the meantime, don't let anyone know who you are, and don't let anyone see you! The Duke of Motta has unleashed a dog, who immediately started to beat the bushes. You know him. It's Matteo Lo Vecchio. Be on your guard.'

He made a sign. One of those mysterious men blindfolded Andrea again and lead him out. There he found Zi' Rosario by his side, who took him by the hand and guided him back along the same way they had come before. When he arrived near Monte di Pietà, he took the blindfold off Andrea. 'Come on,' he said, 'let's hurry on home.'

They took the same way, without talking. Andrea was overwhelmed by what he had seen, and asked himself what reason that mysterious, terrible court could have for taking an interest in the Duke of Motta's acts of usurpation. It certainly was not to avenge anyone's death. So what was it then? And who were those men whom everyone talked about and no one knew, yet who inspired so much terror in the city, often making the magistrate hesitant and timid when he was about to deliver a sentence?

The sect that spread terror of its acts of justice in Palermo and also Val di Mazaro in those years had branches reaching far and wide, which were known only to the supreme tribunal that governed it. Those affiliated with the sect did not know how many they numbered. Each of the members only knew the comrade who had mysteriously led him there blindfolded, and saw only masked men in front of him. Then the members were watched by the leaders, without knowing it and without the possibility of being on their guard. That made them silent, cautious, faithful, and ready, even for sacrifice.

To the poor, to the weak, the sect presented itself as a formidable protector, and that earned it sympathies and that oblivious, yet deeply powerful, solidarity which made the members feel as if they were never alone, and could count on the help and protection of the common people and the lower middle class.

The masters of the State were the nobles and the clergy, because they possessed the wealth. All of the official appointments were in their power; the most delicate offices were awarded only to the nobles, who, naturally, due to caste spirit, helped, supported, and protected each other. Whatever violence they might commit, they were sure of impunity. The most serious sentences were limited to exile or forced residence in some castle belonging to a nobleman or to the royal family, where they were lodged and served with all the comforts, and enjoyed the most complete freedom. But the common people and the lower middle class had only poverty and servitude. The law struck them with the most ferocious punishments that the insane severity of those times placed in its hands, not only to punish real cases of guilt, but also to allow the commission of acts of violence and injustice.

The Blessed Paulists appeared to be and were in fact like a moderating force of reaction. They arose to defend and to protect the weak, and to prevent acts of injustice and violence. They were a State within a State, formidable because hidden, terrible because it judged with no appeals, punished with no mercy, struck without fail. And no one knew who its judges and executors of justice were. They seemed to belong to myth more than reality. They were everywhere, they heard everything, they knew everything, but no one knew exactly where they might be, where they gathered. The discharge of their office as guardians and vindicators was revealed by means of warnings, letters that mysteriously arrived. The man they reached knew he had a death sentence hanging over his head.

How did they arise? Where?

A mystery. They had forefathers – those terrible 'vindicators,'[3] who in the times of Arrigo VI and Federico II were spread over the kingdom. Their leader was a nobleman, Adinolfo di Pontecorvo, their proselytes were in the thousands, and their charge was to vindicate the acts of violence suffered by the weak.

But no one ever discovered who the leader of the Blessed Paulists might be, or could ever say if he belonged to this class or another, this caste or another. No trial could ever, in over a quarter of a century, clear up the mystery. Sometimes a man would climb to the gallows, accused of a bloody murder. People said, people thought for sure, that he was a member. But neither torture nor the sight of the gallows could tear the secret out of him. The law cut off a few branches. But the tree remained and sprouted new shoots.

In 1713 the sect was in full force. It seemed filled with fervour about what it perceived as the work of justice, and it was as if the city was overcome by it. The viceroy government, the high court, and the tribunal of the Holy Offices had united together, putting aside their usual quarrels over pre-eminence and prerogatives, in order to eradicate the sect, but to no avail. At the point when the boldest detectives thought they were on their tracks, they mysteriously died.

This was the secret society that Andrea had run into. This was the tribunal he asked for vendetta. And in his imagination he aggrandized those men through their masks, giving them almost extraordinary appearances. If he had been able to hide and to see the faces of those terrible men who, once he had gone, removed their masks, he would have been astonished by the sight of their plain, common features.

The man who was sitting next to the leader and had asked Andrea some questions was Don Girolamo Ammirata.

[Translator's note: With the customary letter that arrives in a cloud of mystery, Blasco da Castiglione has been summoned to a meeting with the Blessed Paulists, after foiling a crucial part of their plan to perform justice. When he refuses to promise not to interfere again, they quite literally lock him in 'reflection,' their name for the dank, dark subterranean cell where he is left to think about his position. The secret society's leader suddenly appears at the door, and the following scene ensues.]

Part III, chapter VII

The leader of the Blessed Paulists smiled with a sense of commiseration and said, 'You are young, inexperienced in many things, even though you've lived through plentiful experiences of life's misfortunes. The death of the Duke of Motta is not our wish. Indeed, whether he lives or dies is all the same to us. We want the title and patrimony to be returned to their legitimate owner. If first we did not take back from him what he stole by murder, the day he fell beneath the sword of our justice the entire patrimony would pass legally and by full right to his young daughter, Violante, and would not return to Emanuele. Emanuele would remain the victim of a civil death. He would be nothing other than an anonymous nephew of Don Girolamo Ammirata and the theft, the bloodstained robbery, would be sanctioned by an injustice that would be clad in full legal garb. No, no. We have respected the life of Don Raimondo only so that he himself would recognize Emanuele, and give him back what is his.'

Blasco was thinking about Violante. He could not deny to himself that what the other man wanted was nothing but the most rigorous, exact justice. An orphan has been stripped of everything, and it was necessary to give him back what was his. That was the just, proper thing to do. But Blasco was thinking precisely that this act of restitution meant that another innocent person, Violante, would be stripped of everything and disgraced, which he saw as another injustice. In fact, what fault was it of hers that she was born to that man? What misdeed did she commit to warrant being both deprived of the riches which, from the moment of her birth, she had acquired by right and forced to expiate her father's disgrace? This idea stirred up a smouldering feeling of rebellion. Yet he did not dare deny the justice of the Blessed Paulists.

'For the love of justice, we shouldn't be unjust.'

'Toward whom?'

'Toward a person bearing no guilt.'

'What is a man compared to a right that is violated? What is a human life compared to justice that moves straight along its path? So much the worse for those who put themselves across its path. It must go forward, and will crush those it encounters. An innocent is crying? That person's tears compensate those of other innocent people who have cried before. Justice must not have mercy. It must not consider the consequences. Too many tears have been shed. A beautiful, rich, young woman was struck by an atrocious grief when her husband was stolen from her, while she brought the fruit of his blood into the world. Ensnared in a fatal trap, driven to desperation, she died of terror in a stranger's bed, taken in out of charity. A faithful, devoted maid was murdered. The people who took in the baby, orphaned twice over, who hid him and saved him from death, who performed this admirable act of charity, now live on the run like wolves, hiding, forced to defend their life day by day. Another person moans in prison, suffering the infamy of torture that he does not deserve. Two men, guilty only of gathering the ghastly testimonies about the murder, were sent to the gallows, like two common criminals. What are the tears of one innocent victim compared to the blood of eight victims who were innocent too? Justice must follow its own course. No one will stop it, and you, Blasco da Castiglione, even less than the others!'

Blasco heard those words fall upon his ears one by one, cold, implacable. His sense of reason approved of them, but his heart did not and rebelled. And there was something, even in what he approved of, that bolstered that rebellion.

'Why,' he said, 'why, if you're so convinced of the justice of your cause, do you all hide? Why don't you carry on the fight with your faces out in the open? Do noble causes need to hide in the shadows? Therefore, there is something less than noble that forces you to hide. You don't dare face the light, because you feel the faith in your justice wavering!'

'Oh no!' the leader of the Blessed Paulists sharply interrupted. 'Only our faith in legal justice wavers. Actually, it doesn't waver. We have absolutely no faith in it at all, you should have said. And the shadows? They're necessary. They are our strength and our safety. The king's justice is administered by men who see it not as a duty, but as a source of income. They don't deliberate and recognize each person's right. Instead, they guarantee the right of the strongest people over the weakest. The strong ones are the feudal landholders, the State officials, the nobles, and the clergy. Enveloped in immunity, bristling with privileges, the law in their pockets, they have a right as far as they're concerned, that is not the right of others, of the weak. The magistrates and the laws defend precisely this special, privileged right, which is, on the contrary, an abuse and injustice for the masses of the weak, the majority of the people. A knight who kills someone finds in that right and in those magistrates a compassion and tolerance that would appear unshakable. One of the common people who commits the same crime dies on the gallows with great fanfare! A nobleman can take things from his vassal – his livestock, his weapons, his horse – just because he is a vassal. And the nobleman's right allows him to do it. This same right sends that vassal to the gallows if he dares to steal a stack of his master's wheat or a lamb. And this is called justice!

'A poor widow owes money. The creditor can take away her home and throw her out in the middle of the street, and justice gives him a strong hand. In contrast, a nobleman can thrash his creditors and even have them put in prison, and he finds magistrates who deem that this is in conformity with the law. And this too is called justice! Don Raimondo can murder, steal, suppress, and still merit encomiums and rewards, and be placed in a position to administer justice. Don Girolamo Ammirata, who is defending one of the weak, must hide instead, according to the law, so he won't lose his life. And this too is called justice! It is the justice of the State. It is justice according to the laws written for the benefit of the strongest. But this justice is the most monstrous iniquity of all!

'Our justice is not written in any royal constitution, but it is carved in our hearts. We observe it and force others to observe it. We don't have any soldiers, guards, henchmen, corporals. We don't pay judges. We don't search through the legal codes for frivolous arguments to cocreate an honest appearance for injustice. We open our ears and hearts to the voices of the weak, of people who don't have the strength to break the tightly woven net of domination in which they struggle in vain, of people who thirst for justice and ask for it in vain, and suffer.

'Who recognizes our authority? No one. Who recognizes our right to administer justice? No one. Well then, we must impose this authority and this right, and we have only one weapon – terror – and one means to make use of it – mystery, shadows. We don't hide out of cowardice, but out of necessity. The shadows multiply our troops and rouse the faith of those who invoke our protection. A person who wouldn't dare appeal to a legal magistrate to defend himself, his home, the honour of his women, because the appeal would expose him to the wrath, retaliation, and vendettas of the baron or the abbot, in the shadows willingly confides his pain and the violence suffered. A man whom he doesn't see, doesn't know, receives his complaint. We see if he's right. A mysterious warning reaches the domineering malefactor in his own mansion, and the colluding magistrate at his court bench. Do they heed it? We seek nothing more. Do they scorn the warning, and commit further acts of domination, repeating the offence? We punish them and vindicate the offence. No one sees the arm of punishment, no one can escape it. This is our justice. It has never punished an innocent person, and has dried many tears.'

Blasco listened to him in ever-growing amazement. The man became more and more inflamed as he spoke. It seemed as if all of the injustices were passing right before his eyes, injustices that were permitted and fomented by an old social constitution in which human will had taken the place of justice, and by feeble jurisprudence, obstructed by prerogatives, privileges, exemptions, and differences between magistrates or courts. He continued, his voice full of emotion, 'Why don't you, valiant, brave, loyal, and generous as you are, enter the thick of life in the city and in the lands of the barons, as I have? Oh, you'd see how many tears, how much blood, how many acts of infamy it's made of. Then you'd think that not just one of these tribunals but a hundred of them would be necessary to prevent the abuses of power, the violence, and villainous acts of the powerful. I know all of life's miseries. I've penetrated the dens of the peasants, real flocks of slaves bent beneath the blows. I've penetrated the houses of artisans, who barely eke out a living. I've seen the poverty people hide in shame, waiting for nighttime to search through the garbage for a piece of stale bread, a bone, or an apple core. I've seen every kind of human suffering and a hundred, a thousand, ten thousand mouths sobbing and begging for justice! And so I called men of good will together around me, and told them, "We shall defend the weak and the poor!"

'Until the world has changed, while there are still privileged men on one side for whom everything is permitted, with the laws made for their benefit, and men on the other side, condemned to suffer all the wilful acts and all the violent deeds, it is necessary to create a force that opposes, stops, and prevents these wilful acts. It is like a balance of forces. And it's not anything new. Do you perhaps believe that the Blessed Paulists just now came into being? Are you familiar with the history? At the time of Emperor Federico, Adinolfo di Ponte Corvo founded the society of the Vindicators. Its intentions were not different from ours. The Blessed Paulists descend from the *Vindicators*. The Blessed Paulists are centuries old. Sometimes they slumber. Then suddenly, when they've had all they can stand, they awaken. We will die and then others will come after us, because the weak will always need people who protect them, people who defend them. You yourself, Balsco da Castiglione, with all of your courage, with all of your valour, are one of the weak.'

'Me?'

'You're alone, and so you are weak. You're a seed tossed into a field by a baron's caprice and domineering will. Without a name, without a future, you're exposed by your very nature to other domineering men's persecution, forced to hide like a bandit. Perhaps you'd already be dead by now if a hidden, vigilant force hadn't protected you, if we didn't see in you the man who could be the strongest pillar of the sect.'

'Oh no! Never!' yelled Blasco.

'Don't be over hasty!' the leader of the Blessed Paulists coldly replied. 'You've rendered more than one service to our tribunal without even knowing it, though sometimes we were forced to be severe. Even this time, despite your refusal, you've served us.'

'Me?'

'Yes, you. By accepting our invitation.'

'How?'

'But don't you realize that we've eliminated you? Don't you realize you're leaving us an open field?'

He took a watch out of his vest pocket, looked at the time, and added, 'It's already eight o'clock in the evening. At this hour, the Duchess of Motta and Violante are travelling far away.'

'Oh, good Lord!' yelled Blasco, drawing a pistol from his pocket. 'Tell me you're lying!'

'I'm not lying! The duchess and her daughter were put on a boat an hour ago, on my orders.'

'Scoundrel!' yelled Blasco, and he fired the pistol.

The shot thundered in the cavern and smoke filled the air. A laugh replied. Blasco watched in amazement as the leader of the Blessed Paulists yelled loudly towards the door, 'It's nothing! Get away from the door, everyone!' Then he bent down and picked something up off the ground. Holding it out to the young man, he said calmly, 'My good young man, choose some different bullets. These ones, you see, get dented. Farewell!'

He started to leave, but Blasco blocked his way, saying, 'You won't leave this room until I rip off your mask. I want to look you in the face. I want to know that when I tell you you're a coward, my words will strike your skin and not be broken by that artificial face.'

'Is it really so important for you to know who I am?'

'Yes!'

'I could save you the trouble of taking off my mask, but it's useless. You know me.'

'The mask! The mask!'

'Well then, yes. It's better that way. There.' With a quick wave of his hand he removed the black mask from his face.

'Coriolano!' yelled Blasco, 'Coriolano!'

His arms fell to his sides, his voice grew weak, and he felt his knees giving out.

'You! You! You!' he said over and over again despairingly.

'Yes, it is I. What are you so surprised about? You should have suspected it. Me, the person you aimed and shot at!'

Blasco bowed his head, not knowing what to reply. His heart was torn and troubled by two different, conflicting thoughts that could be summed up with two names: Violante and Coriolano.

'What have you done? And what have I done?' he murmured in a voice of unspeakable pain. Then, changing his tone and holding his other pistol out to Coriolano, he added with feverish exaltation, 'Kill me! I beg you, kill me!'

'Why? What's gotten into you? What you did is, I would say, legitimate, as is what I'm doing. I don't bear you a grudge. In your place, I'd have done the same thing. Shake my hand.'

He was forced to reach out for Blasco's hand, and take it in his. Then Blasco, overcome by emotion, burst into sobs, murmuring, 'Oh Violante! Violante!' There was such deep pain in that wail that Coriolano della Floresta was shaken.

'What are you afraid of?' he said. 'I swear on my honour that she doesn't run any danger. Not a hair on her head will be touched. But we need her. Emanuele must be freed and put somewhere he'll be safe from any possible attempt on his life. We won't achieve this without keeping Don Raimondo della Motta's wife and daughter as hostages.'

'And what if he doesn't give in?' asked Blasco with trepidation.

Coriolano was silent for a while.

'Aren't you going to answer me?'

'It would be very serious,' replied the Chevalier della Floresta.

'Aha! Then you see that your promise is subordinated to ... '

'No. I swore on my honour that neither the young woman nor the duchess will suffer the slightest violence, except for the restrictions on their freedom. They will be shut up inside a castle, but treated with all of the regard due their station.'

Blasco seemed tormented by some thought. After a moment of silence, he said, 'What if I were to guarantee not only Emanuele's freedom, but also the recognition of his station and the restitution of his title and patrimony?'

'You, Blasco?' the Chevalier della Floresta exclaimed, stupefied.

'Yes, me. If I were to guarantee this, would you have any difficulty entrusting me with the two women of the House of Albamonte?'

'Make sure you understand the obligation you're assuming, Blasco!'

'I know what I'm saying.'

'Then do you have the power to do this?' asked Coriolano with a penetrating look.

'I do.'

He spoke the words with such certainty that Coriolano looked at him with growing astonishment. What could make Blasco so sure of it? Had he perhaps become close with Donna Gabriella again, and was thinking of making use of her to succeed? He did not think that could be enough to give the young man such a sense of certainty, because Don Raimondo had never let his wife lead him along by the nose. So what was there? It was not necessary to refuse Blasco's proposal, but he did not believe he could entirely agree to it either. There was only one course to take.

'Do you want a truce?' he asked.

'We could even have a truce ...'

'For how long?'

'The time it takes to go to Turin and come back.'

'Spare yourself the trip. The Duke of Motta will be coming here instead.'

'He'll be coming here?'

'In fifteen days, twenty at the most, he'll know his family is in our power.'

'And during all this time, what of that poor young creature?'

'She won't suffer the slightest discomfort. I told you.'

Blasco bent his head, thinking about Violante, and a painful sense of dismay wrung his heart. His voice mixed with regret, pain, and anger, he murmured, 'Oh why, why is it you standing in front of me, and not an enemy, or even a stranger?'

Coriolano smiled and put his mask back on, saying seriously, 'Blasco, here inside, just two men have seen my face – you and Don Girolamo Ammirata. No one else. Those twenty brothers who are in the other room know only this mask, even though they are the leading members of the society. For the other members, I'm a myth. Neither in here nor outside of here, not even when we are alone, may the slightest hint of this escape your lips!'

'Do you want me to promise my most scrupulous silence?'

'No, I know you. Now, wait here until I send someone to get you. And most important of all, obey me.'

He went out, leaving the young man overwhelmed by a thousand ideas, a thousand feelings, that churned in his mind and disturbed him to the core of his being. The tribunal of the Blessed Paulists was still assembled. The men had laid down their masks for a moment and were talking among themselves. A few of them standing tightly around Don Girolamo Ammirata were having him tell all the details about how the attempted kidnapping of Violante had ended in vain. He had had a narrow escape. But Andrea had been stabbed. If the sword had struck him an inch lower, it would have sent him to his maker.

'That young man is some devil, I'm telling you ...'

At that moment, Coriolano went back into the crypt and complete silence fell all at once. Everyone put their masks back on and took their places again. The Chevalier della Floresta said, 'We have a new brother. May each one of you help him and protect him if you see he's in danger.'

A moment later, Blasco was taken into the room again. Caught unawares by Coriolano's invitation, he had to swear his loyalty and silence, according to the oath. One by one, each of the brothers went up to him and embraced him, then pierced his own arm and made the sign of a small cross on Blasco's forehead with the drop of blood. They went back to their places, and the report on deeds and complaints that they had gathered began. Misery cried out through the mouths of those men, whose masks made them immobile, and impassible as marble. Most of the complaints were about the collection of the 'donation' deliberated by Parliament, which, as usual, burdened only the common people. One hundred thousand scudi[4] was the tax burden on milling wheat. The city states had another tax burden of nearly one hundred thousand scudi. Forty thousand was the burden on Palermo, one hundred thirty thousand on the merchants, and twenty thousand on the clerks. In contrast, the barons had a tax burden of only fifty thousand scudi, and the clergy, less than seven thousand. So the taxes paid by the owners of all of the land and all of the wealth in the kingdom, the nobility and the clergy, did not amount to even one-third of what the have-nots were forced to pay. And the owners wrung this light contribution out of the peasants' blood by means of their officials, overseers, and strong-arm henchmen, using every kind of oppression. An entire history of cases of extortion, kidnapping, seizures of collateral, forced property sales that turned the poor people out of house and home, for they could not pay for themselves or the money owed by the baron and the convent for which he was vassal, passed mournfully time after time through the crypt, which seemed shut off from the world. There were also complaints against bloodsucking moneylenders, judges who gave in to friendships or corruption, inhuman and greedy officials, who tried to wring something more out of the victims, for their own profit.

Blasco listened, and out of his dismay he felt an emptiness well up inside him. Life appeared in a very different light and an entire world he had never suspected materialized before his eyes. And Parliament, which assembled with so much solemn pomp and seemed to be the defence and guarantee of the kingdom and the object of everyone's jealousy, now appeared to be the accomplice in all the plundering.

It was almost morning when the tribunal adjourned its session. The Blessed Paulists went out one at a time, mysteriously vanishing in the shadow of a passageway. When everyone was outside, Coriolano said to Blasco, 'Let's go.'

But instead of following the same path the others had taken, he lead Blasco down a passage with a small, secret door that opened onto a stairway. On the landing, an oil lamp burned in front of a Madonna painted on slate. Blasco noticed that though he had had to go down when he had entered the first time, now, as they left, instead of going back up they were going down again. At the end of the stairway was a wide vestibule, closed off by a main door. Coriolano took a key out of his pocket and opened the small, low wicket. He went out first and then had Blasco follow, and shut the door again.

'You see,' he said smiling, 'we're under the protection of the law. This house we've come out of belongs to a judge.'

In fact, it was Judge Baldi's house, on the street that leads from San Cosmo to Capo.

NOTES

1 Vittorio Amedeo di Savoia entered Palermo on 10 October 1713 to take possession of the Kingdom of Sicily, conceded by Filippo V following the Treaty of Utrecht.

2 Zi' is an abbreviated form of *zio*, literally meaning uncle, but often used as an informal title of respect in parts of southern Italy.

3 The *vindicosi*, or vindicators, are described as a historical sect by Francesco Maria Emanuele e Gaetani Villabianca (1720–1802) in his *Diari palermitani* (Palermo diaries). According to this author, they may date back to 1185.

4 A scudo was a large silver or gold coin used at the time. This form of currency varied in appearance and value according to the region of Italy in which it circulated and the historical period.

Testagrossa Agrees

GIUSEPPE ERNESTO NUCCIO

I

Testagrossa[1] cracked open his eyes, got the kinks out of his numb legs, and stretched his arms. His right hand hit the column hiding him from view, so he exclaimed 'Out of my way!' The sun was just rising above the sea, turning the domes in the Martorana and the carved moulding of the Palazzo di Città golden. The first carts and carriages for hire were passing by. The carters' singsong, roosters' crowing, and pealing bells ran through the air, mingling as they welcomed the dawning day.

Testagrossa sucked in his stomach, slipped through the tight space, grabbed onto the edge of the column's base, and dropped onto the steps of the University. Three somersaults, one right after the other, and he had all of the kinks out of his body. Then he took off at a run towards the small fountain that had sparkling clear water. But then along came a carriage, and the scamp scrambled on in a leap, happy because it was heading towards Porta Sant'Antonio. It was taking him right to his spot, so he spread his arms to grip the springs, and threw back his head, as if posing for a portrait. What a peculiar figure would have appeared! A head big and round as a ripe watermelon on a tiny, painfully thin body, and his tiny body swimming in a huge cloak, as if it were hung on two crossed sticks. From a distance he looked like a scarecrow, like the ones you see in the vineyards at harvest time.

But his flat face, with its wide mouth, squashed nose, and laughing, cat-green eyes, was always poised for a snicker with hints of gaiety and mockery that made the police agents' reprimands die on their lips when they caught him making mischief in the streets.

Turning into Via Lincoln, the carriage arrived near Porta Castrofil-
ippo, and Testagrossa jumped off. In a flash he popped into Piazza
Magione, where the fruit market was. The huge piazza was bordered
mostly by one-storey houses. Here and there, groups of men were
standing under wide canopies around heaps of large baskets spilling
out all sorts of ripe fruit. While everything around the city was sleeping, that piazza was buzzing joyfully with a beehive of industrious,
fast activity. At every opening you ran into carts drawn by mules,
some coming from the fields loaded with fruit, and some empty,
coming to load up. Still others were headed off with rosy peaches,
yellow apricots, deep red cherries, and pears and apples, whose
perfume sent a welcome hint of the sunny countryside into the air,
taking them to the fruit shops in the city, the port, or the train station,
where they left for cold countries.

Testagrossa approached a group of men and then got on his hands
and knees. Slipping between their legs, he popped up right in the
middle of all the baskets as if he had sprung out of the ground.

'Oh! Here's Testagrossa,' said a fruit vendor. 'We were just starting
to get worried about you.'

'I got back from the theatre late last night. I slept in a bit.'

'Shut up, Pasquino,' the auctioneer yelled at him, giving him a cuff
on the head.

He started up the sale again. Twelve baskets of ripe peaches, so
plump they looked as if their pink skin were ready to burst, were on
auction. The auctioneer was standing on a basket turned upside down
in order to have a clear view of all the fruit vendors, who were careful
to watch him steadily, with their faces turned up and eyes stock still.
His eyes were moving constantly, quickly looking at all of them one by
one, and as if reciting a rosary, he loudly and continuously translated
the bids that the buyers made without a sound, just giving a sign with
their open fingers.

The peaches were given to the highest bidder, and then had to be
weighed on the scale. That was when Testagrossa's work was needed.
As he would do every morning, he took the basket by one handle, and
with the help of the buyer, who grabbed the other handle, he lifted it
up onto the hook of the scale. When the basket had been weighed,
Testagrossa spotted the most beautiful peach and stuck it in his roomy
pocket. The fruit was what they paid him for his labour. So there were
twelve baskets weighed, and twelve plump peaches that the boy put
in his roomy pocket, which went all the way around the inside of his

jacket. Then baskets of cherries were sold at auction too. After the hard work of lifting those really heavy baskets up high, he took his handfuls of fruit, which joined what he already had.

When the fruit market closed and little by little the piazza emptied of people, carts, and baskets, Testagrossa's knapsack-like pocket was so loaded that the weight pulled his jacket way down and his pointed shoulders threatened to break through. In fact, on account of all the weight, he had a hard time dragging himself towards the main entrance of a building. He threw himself down on the first step, half-dead from exhaustion and broken in two by a pain in his back, as if he had fallen off a tiled roof and hit his backbone on a sharp pebble. But, in any case, he felt that pain every morning until later on, when little by little it went away and all he had left was the fruit or the money he earned selling it.

After digging all the pieces of fruit out of his pocket, Testagrossa arranged it beautifully on the marble step. There were twelve really plump peaches and a deep red, shiny mountain of cherries lined by green stems. But just at the moment when the boy was enjoying his wealth, the small door to the doorkeeper's quarters bursts open and a big woman with a face like a full moon and a hairy double chin appears in the doorway. Noticing the boy peacefully lying down as if he were in his own home, she yelled at him in a deep, ogreish voice, 'You brazen little thief! Who'd you swipe this stuff from? Get it out of here! If you don't, I'll kick you out.'

'Oh! So angry, zia.[2] A little patience. If you give me some time, I can explain.'

'What do you have to explain, you gargoylish imp! Did you steal it? Well, I don't want to know anything about it. But get it out of here.'

'But if you give me time, I'll explain ...'

The woman lost her patience and went furiously back inside. She reappeared brandishing an enormous ladle, and advanced threateningly on the scamp. He stayed there perfectly still, as if made of stone, with that bursting, hearty laugh on his wide face. The woman, disarmed by the scamp's imperturbable look, softened her voice and asked, 'Well then, are you going to move or not? Are you waiting for some fellow tenant? So, speak up then!'

'Now I'll explain. Right this instant. I'm not going to move because I'm really tired. My back's in pieces. And I didn't steal this fruit. I'm the produce weigher, and so it's mine, all mine.'

'Okay. But you're making my steps all messy. If someone needs to come up or go down, they won't know where to step.'

'I'll rest just a little more, and I'll slip away.'

'And what do you do with the fruit?'

'What do I do with it? I sell it.'

'How much do you want for it?'

'How much do I want? So, how much do I want? There are twelve peaches. They weigh around two kilos. There's over a kilo of cherries. Four, eight, twelve – I'll settle for half a lira.'

'I'll give you eight soldi. There's certainly not a full two kilos.'

'Done! Eight soldi. But I want this peach here, and I want this handful of cherries.'

'Go ahead.'

When the sale was concluded, the doorkeeper said to Testagrossa, 'Hooray! I like you. When you're hungry, I'd love to give you a bowl of soup.' As she dismissed him, she gave him a smack that was as kind as a hug.

II

Sitting cross-legged on the ground, Testagrossa was crunching on a sandwich when someone snuck up on him on tiptoe, and planted himself right in front of him. Without moving, Testagrossa looked stealthily at the body, and saw some incredibly long thing. 'Damn it! He's everywhere I turn, like death. He won't leave me alone!' thought the scamp.

It was Serpenera, recognizable by his never-ending feet and long, blackened claws.

'You must be really hungry if you're eating so early,' said Serpenera.

'Yeah,' replied Testagrossa without looking up.

'Where've you been? Haven't seen you in a long time. There's so much news I've gotta tell you about. Come on, get up!'

'I'm really tired.'

The long legs bent, and Serpenera sat down next to Testagrossa.

'I tracked down a place to sleep. It's a palace. And you can stay there ... and a hundred other fellows too. But not only that. There are some extra clothes and some extra pairs of shoes. There'd be a suit and a pair of shoes for you too. New ones, though, not something off a dead guy. You'd look like a young gentleman, not some scoundrel. Gosh! Those are quite some rags you've got on. With the others instead, you'd look like Florio's[3] son in person.'

Testagrossa was busy nibbling at his sandwich and thought, 'H'm! You're not going to get me. I know you, you hoodlum! You want me to be in your same dirty business!'

'You see,' he went on, 'I amuse myself all day long. Hear what beautiful music.' And he hit his pocket with his knuckles, making some coins jingle.

'What would I ever do with it?' said Testagrossa, shrugging his shoulders. 'I eat too. Look!' And he took one bite out of his sandwich and another one out of his peach. 'But I'm not scared of ... anyone.'

'What do you mean by that?' threatened the awful boy.

'What do I mean? Me? Nothing.'

'So then is it true?'

'What's true?'

'It's true you're a *muffutu*.'[4]

'Ah! Ah!' Testagrossa burst out laughing. 'I'm not a *muffutu* because I don't care about ...'

'Then listen to me.' Serpenera's voice turned soft, flattering. His mouth, which was resting against Testagrossa's ear, gave off a stench of crushed cigar butts. 'You have to be one of ours. I'm telling you this for your own good. Because do you know what the fellows have gotten into their heads? They've gotten it in their heads that you're a *muffutu*. I've always taken your side. And if someone treats you bad, they have to answer to me. But for the moment, if they saw you were with us, they wouldn't think about it anymore. As long as I'm around, don't be scared.'

'Pooh! Me, I'm not even scared of Orlando!'[5]

'But, besides that, listen to me. If you come in with us guys, you'll have as much pasta, bread, wine, and money as you want. And what does it take? Nothing. A steady eye, light fingers, the face of a half-wit, and everything runs magnificently.'

Testagrossa was busy crunching on his sandwich and looking at the crystal clear blue sky. No, he was not paying any mind to what Serpenera was insinuating. He felt such a strong dislike for that awful boy, with a face like a fox and slimy, blackened fingers like the paws of some filthy animal, that he could hardly keep his hands under control. It would have given him such enormous satisfaction to shower punches on that mug of his. How many wicked things he had seen him do and how many times he had seen him bullying the poor street urchins at the train station, the port, the market! Even if that boy had offered him a treasure, he would have refused it because of the strong repulsion rushing through his veins.

'The other day at the Ciaculli fair,' continued Serpenera with his stinking breath, 'a box of sweets just happened to fall into our hands. It looked like sweets, but when you lifted it up it weighed a ton. Were weights for a scale inside, maybe? Take a guess, Testagrossa! If you're good at it, just guess what was inside. We opened it. And what was inside? There was a small bag so full of coins it was ready to burst. There were silver coins too. Get it? And there were more of the white coins than the black.[6] Just imagine what luxury! See what strokes of luck happen when you're with other people ... I'll introduce you to my friends and to ... Don Lucio ... the "maestro." Then you'll see for yourself.'

But now that Testagrossa's eyes had gotten used to the sight of him, he looked furtively at Serpenera's face and mouth. His lips were droopy and almost bluish, like the lips of people who've just died, and his big, blackish teeth looked like the Saracens' in the puppet show.

'So you see what a lucky turn of chance!' insisted Serpenera, grabbing Testagrossa's arm and shaking the boy, as if to make him pay attention.

'A lucky turn of chance ... with someone's hand in it,' said Testagrossa in a malicious, grating drawl. 'But you'd better not tell anyone about it.'

Serpenera furrowed his brows and clenched his teeth. Then, pretending he did not understand, he asked, his voice mixed with threatening and coaxing tones, 'Well, are you coming in with us?'

'No, I'm not coming in with you. I don't want to come with you.'

Serpenera stood up, pulling Testagrossa along by the arm. He pushed him towards the wall and stared him grimly in the eyes.

'Careful! I'll be the first to beat you to death,' and he raised his fist up, ready to strike. But Testagrossa laughed scornfully in his face. Furious, the other boy punched him in the head – one, two, three times. Then the two entangled bodies lurched a few steps, leaned over and toppled down, and rolled around on the ground. They suddenly stood up, freeing themselves, and then became more tightly entangled again, until Serpenera managed to trap the boy in the large circle of his arms. He pushed him over to the wall with two violent shoves. Half-dazed, Testagrossa dropped his arms to his sides, and the other boy seized the opportunity to grab him around the neck and pin him up against the wall. He stared him grimly in the eye and shouted in his face, 'To me you're just a little worm ... I'll swallow you with one peck. Are you coming?'

Testagrossa gathered all his strength and gave a shove to get out of the boy's tight hold. But the awful boy, his eyes red and lips even darker, pushed him back against the wall with the entire strength of his body, planting his big feet on the ground. Then he paused a bit, as if to catch his breath, but without relaxing his grip around the other boy's neck, which was throbbing beneath his hand like a small frightened heart.

'Do you want to come with us? Or do you still want to act like Rodomonte?'[7]

But Testagrossa could not hear him, because a deep screeching like the sound of a car about to break down was rolling through his poor head. Meanwhile, Serpenera had pulled out a knife with his right hand. Resting the tip of it on his pants, he had made the small pointed blade fly out.

'Talk ...'

Feeling ready to faint, Testagrossa struggled furiously and let out a piercing scream. The other boy stabbed him and ran away. Freed from the tight grip, the boy fell to the ground on his back.

III

Testagrossa groped along the ground and then leaned against the wall, slowly getting on his feet. He felt just like someone in a shipwreck, who had been knocked around by the ship and then whirlpools, and finally washed onto a reef by a furious storm. All his limbs ached, but most of all, he still felt like he was suffocating, as if he had been underwater a long time and it was still hard to breathe. So, as if seeking the open air, he dragged himself haltingly along, leaning against the Villa Giulia's long iron grating, towards the seashore, where he collapsed on the quay and closed his eyes slightly against the unbearable brightness of the sparkling blue sea. He breathed in large gusts of fresh air, greatly restoring his body and soul.

The open sea was calm, a beautiful indigo colour that shaded off into emerald green, with bands of silvery rivulets now and then, and panted under the sun's white caress. The entire shore, from Cape Zafferano to Mount Pellegrino, hugged the sea in the large cradle of its arms, bejewelled by villages sparkling luminously white.

But the sun's kiss was too strong, and Testagrossa felt an intense burning on his head, so he stood up. Moving less slowly than before, as his legs recovered their usual energy, he came back towards the city, looking for somewhere cool. He entered the city again through the shady lanes of Kalsa, where the women were sitting near the doors of their hovels embroidering, and their children, half-naked, were playing in the dirt.

Testagrossa stole a look into a poor house. In the doorway, there was a young, fair-skinned woman who was singing. As she sang in the sweetest voice, she lulled her baby to sleep.

Alavo, sleep and rest;
Your crib flies in the middle of the rose.

Just then, a secret, obscure desire for refuge and protection, like the bitter nostalgia for a distant, nebulous childhood, blossomed again in Testagrossa's heart. A distant childhood that he forced himself to see again, steadily training his memory's eye on a dark cloud, lit up now and then by fleeting bolts of lightening. The sudden bursts of light illuminated two images. One was a young, fair-skinned woman with a perennial smile lighting up her good face and a joyful warble in her throat, like a cheerful blackcap's. The other was a bearded man with thick eyelashes over two red eyes – like fires burning beneath bushes – and an ugly, raspy voice like a wolf-man's. Then the tragic vision appeared that, yet again, made him shudder. The vision of the young woman, paler than usual, with a stream of blood on her lips, where the light of her smile remained. Beside this vision was another, of the bearded man, his wicked eyes angrier, who was struggling in a cloud of police agents and people screaming, threatening. Then, as always, an unbearable pang gripped his heart. To escape the strange sick feeling, Testagrossa started running like a madman in search of any group of stray scamps like himself that he could join up with, in order to forget.

He ran across a lot of streets until he reached Piazza Sant'Euno, where there was a group of kids playing toss up. He was welcomed with cheerful slaps, which he returned in kind.

'Do you want to play?'
'Do you have any money on you?'
'How much?'
'You're all scratched up!'
'Were you baptized?'[8]

'I want to play,' was all Testagrossa replied, and he took some coins out of his pocket. As he looked them over again, he saw one that bore a mark from the stabbing. He lifted it to his lips and gave it a smacking kiss, as if it were an amulet or a sacred relic.

'This does miracles,' he said.

'Does it make hunger go away?'

'No, no. It protects you from getting stabbed, like Orlando's shield.'

There was a round of laughter.

'Come on, let's play,' one boy said to him.

'So let's play.'

They played toss-up. Since Testagrossa was the winner, he closed one centesimo in his right hand, then put both hands behind his back so the other boy could not see. He passed the centesimo from one hand to the other several times, finally closing it in his left hand. Then he showed the fellow his closed fists. Putting one fist up to his mouth and then the other, he recited:

Old table, new table,
Where do you discover it, where do you find it?

'Here,' said the other boy, pointing to the right fist. But the centesimo was in the left one, so Testagrossa won a centesimo. They played a bunch of matches, until Testagrossa lost four centesimi.

'I don't want to play Old Table anymore,' he said.

'Let's play heads or tails.'

'No. I don't want to play for money anymore. If not, how will I eat? Besides, tonight I want to go to the Puppet Show.' Testagrossa put an end to it, and ran towards the other kids yelling, 'Let's play the game without money.'

'No, no. Let's play down down pretty swallow.'

Some other little stragglers ran up shouting, and the silent piazza resounded with shouts, songs, and whistles.

Ten boys were picked, the fastest ones. They counted out the boys for each side, and the first five, drawn by lots, were knights. The other five boys were horses. They went over to the wall and bent over, resting their foreheads on the back of their open hands, their palms flat against the stone.

Elected their *mastro* (leader), Testagrossa gave names to the four knights: *Rinninedda* (Little Swallow), *Sceccu d'oru* (Golden Ass), *Aceddu* (Bird), *Liuni* (Lion). Then he got two rocks and put them a short distance behind the horses. He signalled the playmates on his side, and in one leap all five of them saddled up on the backs of the horses and covered their eyes. When Testagrossa was sure that none of the horses could see him, he sang out:

Come down come down Little Swallow,
Go to sound the bell,
Fennel on the mountain,
Fennel on that side,
Come down come down Golden Ass!

The scamp who had the name Golden Ass jumped to the ground and went to sound the bell, that is, to beat the rocks together, and then got back on his horse. Then Testagrossa sang:

Eyes on the mountain,
Everyone turn this way!

At that order, the knights jumped to the ground, switched places in a jumble, and went to stand in front of the horses. The horses stood up, turned around, and looked at the riders, who were jiggling their hands in front their chests as they sang:

Little doughnut, it wasn't me!
Little doughnut, it wasn't me!

The third horse pointed at the right boy, who had the name Golden Ass, and they exchanged places. Golden Ass became a horse, and the other boy was a knight. The game lasted over an hour, with wonderful correctness and discipline, because no one disobeyed the leader's law. When they got tired of playing, the boys went off, each one going his own way.

IV

Back to his usual cheerful self, Testagrossa wandered around quite a long way, until he went into Via Montesanto, where an unusual buzzing coming from Giglio lane caught his attention. He went down the street and saw a bunch of people in Piazza Santa Rosalia. He asked a kid perched on the church's iron fence, 'What's going on?'

'Some young woman died. The band's here. Now the funeral carriage is coming, the one with the gold owls. And the band's going to play.'

Squeezing, pushing, bending down almost on hands and knees, and slipping through the crowd, Testagrossa reached the small open space next to the house where they were supposed to carry down the dead woman. While he was trying to see, standing up straight and craning his neck, he got a hard shove. He turned around and saw a squat man with a huge belly and a big gold chain hanging outside his vest, who was threatening him with his raised fist. Testagrossa was about to make one of his usual faces at him, but then thought it was not the right moment if he wanted to enjoy the music in peace. So he turned back around with a shrug of his shoulders.

Then the crowd swayed, because the big hearse with the gold owls and four black horses was arriving. The scamp got another big shove from the same man with the big chain when he was pushed back against him again by the swaying crowd. This time too he shrugged in an act of saintly resignation. But a throng of scamps running from the lane came up like a company of *bersaglieri*[9] on the attack. Their column bumped into the crowd, a passage opened up and victorious, they flooded the small square.

Then, in that moment, though Testagrossa pushed his hands out in front of him and parried with his fists, he was shoved backwards three or four times, the last one so hard that he slammed against the big belly of the man with the gold chain. The man leaned over and fell with a thud. There was the sound of another hoarse shout, and Testagrossa felt someone grabbing him. He jerked away, freeing himself from the hold, and instinctively, with no idea why he did it, he took off running like a madman. Who knows if that man hurt himself because of him!

At the shout, all the people who were near the stout man rushed up, barely able to help get him back on his feet. The man patted down his entire body, and thought his chain was missing. He caught a glimpse of the scamp running away and started to yell, 'Stop thief! Stop thief!' Lots of people yelled the words over and over again, and seeing as how the man was running, they started to run too, though they didn't have a clue about anything. But because of the man's massive body, though he tried his best to run, he did not get too far. Instead, he was lurching along, huffing and puffing like a bellows, and continuing to yell at the top of his lungs, 'Stop thief!' Thinking that the man had really been robbed, the people shouted too and rushed to help him. By then, a threatening crowd of people was running behind Testagrossa. He crossed the piazza in a leap and a jump, and dashed down Via Stazione, leaving fairly far behind the crowd that was chasing him and redoubling their shouts, 'Stop, stop ....'

Meanwhile, this way and that, and up above, in the doorways, at the windows, on the balconies, people looked out in fright at the sound of all the commotion, and many of them joined the main body of pur-suers. A lot of them could have grabbed Testagrossa, who shot by like an arrow. But thinking that was business for the police, all of them ran along just to enjoy the scene. Nimble as a fawn, Testagrossa crossed Via Garibaldi and Via Magione in a few leaps, and had already reached Piazza Magione. He had gained a lot of ground and heard the shout-ing muffled by the distance, so he turned around to take a look. His fear dissolved into great amusement at the sight of a large crowd of people who, instead of running, were pawing furiously at the ground – like a herd of roped-in horses – around the stout man. As they goaded him to run, as if he had to win a race for a prize, he struggled his hardest to make his huge body move forward. But instead of running, he looked like he was stomping grapes in a vat.

Testagrossa idled around to enjoy the spectacle for a short while. Then he started to run again. Turning, he unexpectedly landed in the doorkeeper's quarters of the big woman who had bought his fruit that morning.

'Zia,' the scamp said, his voice mixed with pitifulness and gaiety, 'they're chasing me. They didn't see me come in. Get in front of the door! Quick, in front of the door! Hide me behind your skirt. They're coming! They're coming!'

In fact, the loud shouts, drawled out and intermixed with the throng's shuffling feet, reached the woman's ears. Without waiting an instant, she went to plant herself in the doorway, leaning her tall body against the door jamb with her right hip, as if she were there to hold up the building. Testagrossa crouched down between her skirt and the wall, carefully peeking out so he too could enjoy the spectacle of the stout man being made fun of. When the wave of people was there in the street, the roar of the voices, echoing against the tall walls, became noisier and louder. The man with the chain stepped in front of every-one, with his face as red as hot embers and his short little arms flap-ping like the wings of a big duck being chased. And the people all around him danced to and fro, more and more agitated, shouting between bursts of laughter they could hardly choke back, 'Stop thieeef, stop thieeef!' And the man kept reciting the refrain, 'He stole my chain, he stole my chain!'

The crowd took great pains to hold back the laughter at the sight of the small gold chain that had come loose from the small left pocket, and was bouncing around below the man's enormous belly. Precisely because of the protuberance of his stomach, he could not see the chain, and thought it had been stolen by the scamp.

People appeared at the windows and doors, and guessing from the uproar what the joke was about, they shouted too, 'Graaab him, graaab him!' Then, attracted by that new racket, swarms of police agents and carabinieri rushed up.

'What happened to you?' a brigadiere[10] asked the stout man.

The man leaned against the wall to catch his breath, and between one pant and another he mumbled, 'Some rascal stole my chain.'

The brigadiere said, 'He must have stolen your watch, perhaps, because the small chain is dangling from your pocket.'

The man patted his fingers over his stomach, pulled out the small chain attached to his watch, looked them over, touched them carefully, and let out a hearty laugh of relief. But mortified, he faced the simultaneous eruption of the entire crowd's laughter.

Testagrossa, who had heard and seen everything, sprang out, did five somersaults in front of the stout man, and off he went, repeating the line 'Stop thieeef! Stop thieeef!'

V

After walking the city streets for a long time, earning a little money by doing other drudging jobs, Testagrossa was reduced to Piazza Rivoluzione, where the soup man, the restaurant owner for stray urchins, was. He squatted on the sidewalk and, in a couple of mouthfuls, wolfed down a good bowl of bean soup that the soup man had given him in exchange for a few soldi. He topped it off with half a litre of fresh water, wiped his face with his big sleeves, lit a long cigar butt, and turned into the lane to read the program for the upcoming show on the poster for the Puppet Theatre.

That evening they were showing *The Council of Agramante*, in which the biggest fleet in the world unites against Charlemagne and his paladins. While Testagrossa craned his neck to look at the picture, which depicted Agramante's royal palace, the shrill sound of the barrel organ came from the Puppet Theatre, located in the middle of the lane. The assiduous theatre-goers came from the two ends of the short, filthy street. The little children came running, shouting and laughing. The older ones, almost men already, approached calmly, swaying back and forth like ducklings after a meal, with their caps tilted to the side of their head and hands stuck in their pants' pockets.

A woman was taking admission money in front of the theatre door, which was half closed and covered by a curtain shining with grease. Testagrossa gave her his money. As he went in, he spotted an empty seat on a bench in the first row, and he perched happily on it. Although the last light of dusk lingered outside, inside it seemed as if it was already night, it was so dark. So Don Gaetano hurried to light the oil lamps.

Then the big curtain with the 'Battle of Roncisvalle,' or rather 'The Massacre of the Paladins,' appeared in all its magnificence. A crazy jumble of soldiers, horses, warriors on their backs, on hands and knees, overturned horse-drawn carts, and a tangle of legs, heads, shields, and swords. In the middle of all that confusion, Rinaldo was raising his terrible long sword in both hands over a group of warriors who surrounded him and threatened him from all sides with thick rows of lances and swords, while Orlando stood atop a hill, his cheeks puffed out and eyes blazing, blowing a horn in despair, to warn Charlemagne about the imminent defeat.

As soon as all the lamps were lit, the smell of oil delighted the little scamps, who were making fun of each other to keep from getting bored during the wait. A hard smack sent Testagrossa's cap flying, and it landed over a lamp at the front of the stage. Testagrossa rushed to get it before it got burned. But as he returned, he saw his place was entirely taken up by a young schmuck with a big lock of tousled hair hiding half his forehead. The boy gave him such a surly look, as if to say 'If you get near me I'll bite your head off,' that Testagrossa thought he would steer clear of him and choose a less conspicuous seat next to a stage pillar, where he could scratch the itchy scruff of his neck. But he cheered up quickly because in his new seat he clearly saw that getting smacked on the head was not his fortune alone. Staring on, he saw lightening fast hands followed by the sharp sounds of smacks wholeheartedly delivered, then angry ouches, and a sudden turning of heads that were struck. A din of shouting arose from that spot, which would have been taken for bedlam if the barrel organ had not picked up the music at just the right time and partly drowned it out with the crazy screeching of a war march.

All of a sudden the organ went silent, and a kid raised a stick high in the air, shouting, 'Let's do the catcall!' The order was passed from one mouth to another. One by one the voices stopped. It became dead silent. Then a faint sound like lots of whimpering children started to rise, becoming louder and louder until it sounded like the piercing meowing of a pack of stray cats at night, turning more and more angry. Then it sounded like a distant stormy sea approaching, until it seemed to join roaring thunder claps that echoed in the valleys of the sky. But the loudest thunder of all, as if lightening had struck inside the hall, was the thunder produced by the furious blows of Don Gaetano's big paws stomping on the wooden floor.

As if frightened, the organ hastily struck up a *sonatina larga*, and the curtain, majestic, raised slowly. And suddenly there appears a splendid royal palace in bright reds and golden and silvery sparkles made of tinfoil. We are in King Agramante's court, and he has summoned the council of his thirty vassal kings.

They come in one by one, throwing one foot in front of the other, plant themselves in the middle of the stage, and make a deep bow to the respectable shirt-sleeved audience seated in the pit. Then they go line up, one next to the other near the stage wings, where their shields are adjusted so the strings do not get tangled up. Afterwards, they stay there, hard, stiff, their big harsh eyes open, and their feet dangling.

Testagrossa smiles in satisfaction at seeing those powerful, incredibly rich kings, who end up just like sausages hanging in the delicatessen. At one point – since the kingdom is populated with kings dressed in purple, ermine, and gold, with crowns, helmets, and pieces of armour that sparkle like suns – a chorus comes from behind the scenes, the voices swelling as if the words were shouted by a mass of people, 'Hooray Agramante!' And suddenly Agramante, the young and powerful king, comes forward, walking haughtily with his head held high and face stern, his chest all puffed out. At each step he stops, and quickly turns his face in jerks, now to the right towards the vassals, and now to the left towards the audience, as if to say, 'I am who I am!,' while he gives a greeting of patronage with his left fist.

The entire theatre is filled with a kind of silence full of awe, expectation, and respect. Agramante stops, suddenly puts his legs together and then spreads them again. He puts his right arm out straight, flexes his knees like a fencing master on the attack, and in Don Gaetano's voice, a thundering, clear, full voice that puts strong emphasis on expressiveness, intones: 'Oh! My able and noble Kings, o pillars of granite and bronze, you who with your powerful arms of iron uphold my throne, which shines so very bright, like the eastern sun, so very grave was the disgrace that the arrogant King Charlemagne did to us, o my able and noble Kings, o pillars of granite and bronze!

'We shall wash this disgrace away with blood! And until we have washed it clean with blood we shall feel ashamed to live in this so very resplendent land of ours!

'Let us gather together, o my most powerful Kings, o pillars of bronze of my kingdom, let us gather together a formidable fleet! Let us form the most formidable fleet in the world! We shall cross the sea and with this formidable fleet we shall go join in battle with arrogant King Charlemagne in his very own dominions.

'And let us swear, o powerful Kings, let us swear that we shall never return until we have first destroyed the entire army of King Charlemagne along with all his paladins.'

'Boom!' yelled Testagrossa from the pit. It was the first sign of general criticism, expressed by all the young spectators with hisses and ironic exclamations.

But King Agramante did not care about the reception that his high intentions were given among the lowly people, who clearly took sides with Charlemagne. Imperturbable, with the same expression of majesty in his every move, he went towards his kings. Shaking their heads one by one, they expressed their complete approval, which was echoed by the chorus of hoorays shouted from behind the scenes, 'Hooray Agramanteee!'

King Agramante ended up near the stage wings, joining the other kings already there, stock still and stiff, staring at box number two. But suddenly old King Suprino with his long beard leaves the line of kings to advise against going to war, because the paladins of France are the bravest warriors on earth and able to throw the strongest army into chaos.

'Bravo! Hooray! Great! Saintly words!' come the shouts from the pit.

But Agramante shakes his head, and one after another the kings do the same as a sign of disdainful reprobation. At this point, like a wounded lion cub, hot-tempered Rodomonte leaps from the line and plunks down on the stage floor with two terrible stomps of his paws that make the whole theatre shake.

'You there!' he yells, exasperated, tossing all about and flailing his legs and arms on all sides. 'You there, King Suprino, old age has made you cowardly in deed and cowardly at heart! Do not listen, o valiant Kings, to this man's bad advice. Take courage! We possess much greater courage than the best paladins of France, and we shall destroy them like a fistful of ...'

'Boom!' shouted Testagrossa. 'Blowhard! Braggadocio!' added others amidst an uproar of infernal shouts and the shrillest hissing ever. Until a boiled potato crumbled on Rodomonte's shining shield. A roaring applause followed, and an overwhelming demand for an encore. But Don Gaetano's threatening face appeared in the wings. The wiser spectators administered a few smacks to the most unruly ones, and calm was restored.

The puppet show resumed, and continued until King Caramante – after giving his advice on the surest means for defeating Charlemagne, that is, to spirit the young Ruggero away from the Castle, enchanted by the sorcerer Atlante, by stealing the ring from Angelica, the Princess of Cathay – willed his own death that very instant, in order to give solid proof of the prophecy. Raving applause exploded at how natural the death of the old wooden king had seemed. In the midst of the applause and whistles the curtain fell.

The woman who had been at the entrance came in to sell pumpkin seeds, boiled potatoes, prickly pears, and water. The yelling had become louder again and was joined by the shouts of impatient customers. Testagrossa also bought a cent's worth of boiled potatoes. But of the three potatoes he got, he was just barely able to eat one, because the other two were suddenly whisked away by greedy hands. He leaned against the pillar and took a look around. It was the usual audience of acquaintances. Over there was the watermelon vendor from Corso dei Mille, with his red scarf tied around his neck in place of a tie. And there, the two shiners from Fieravecchia, with their unmistakable lumpy noses, all shiny and red. Then Brebitebré, whose flat, simpleton face moved people to pity, so he could get handouts on the streets. And there, the apish faces of Guercino and Maruzza, the neighbourhood's notorious petty thieves. The rest were children and older boys, with broad, honest, and happy faces, who were labourers and skipping night school to enjoy the show. Testagrossa had one of them sitting next to him, so sleepy his eyes were barely open.

'What time do you want me to wake you up?' he asked.

The other boy smiled. He was a small labourer, with big blotches of lime dust all over his clothes, on his cap, and even his face.

'I thought I was at night school,' he said. 'I get up at four in the morning, my friend. I go to work at the Falde, and to get there on time ...'

'But I see you here almost every night. So when do you go to night school?'

'When do I go? A couple of weeks at the beginning of the year. And then, instead of going down Via Schiavuzzu that leads to school ... I take Maestri d'Acqua lane, leading to the Puppet Theatre.'

'By now you ought to know a lot more than the teacher!'

'Yeah! I've done three years of first grade, and I'm always stuck there. I always get to the picture of the pipe in the alphabet. Every year I start at the beginning and stop at the pipe. But even if I went, what do you think? As soon as I sit down on the bench and I open my eyes wide and open up my mind to understand what the teacher says, what happens? A veil comes down over my eyes and a heavy sleep ... It must be a sickness. I can't pay attention. I last ten or fifteen days. Then I withdraw and start to attend this school. I don't fall asleep here. In fact, I have a good time. I'd like to know how to read and write. But it's that sickness.'

'But it's really got to be a sickness that spreads. There are more of your schoolmates here than at school. Do they all have this sleep sickness?'

'You don't believe it, but that's how it is. Ask all those guys. They'll tell you the same thing I did. You try hard to pay attention and you get sleepy. So sleepy! Like you hadn't slept for two or three nights!'

'Instead of going to school at night, go during the day. Then it's all solved.'

'There you are! And what about the factory boss who has to give me permission? He won't let me for sure.'

'And why won't he let you?'

'Why? Well, because we work a full day.'

'Right. But what do you care about reading anyway? When there's news in the papers, when they kill someone or something extraordinary happens, you hear everyone talking about it.'

'Oh, listen,' said the small labourer, lowering his voice, 'listen, just a little while ago, when I was on my way here, I found a really, really long knife on the ground. I've got it in my pocket. As soon as the show's over, I'll run to take it home.'

'Good,' said Testagrossa approvingly, 'because if officer Troisi sees you with it, he'll slap you in prison like ...'

VI

The sentence died on Testagrossa's lips. Slouching near the door with a look mixed between sullen and drowsy, was Serpenera's tall, horrid body. He took two steps, stopped, and squinted as he looked incessantly all around, until his eyes lit on Guercino and Manuzza. He wrinkled his nose as he grimaced a satisfied smile, as if he had found exactly whom he was looking for. Then he walked towards the front with long swift steps, placing his big palms heavily on the shoulders of the people sitting there. They jerked around angrily, but put a polite smile on their faces at once, seeing Serpenera, the thief, troublemaker, stabber, with whom nobody wanted to have words.

Sitting on the bench between Manuzza and Guercino was a boy sleeping soundly. Picking him up under his arms, Serpenera went to set him down on the front of the stage, at the risk of him being burned by the flames flickering in the oil lamps, and went back to sit in the empty seat. Testagrossa was trembling. His heart was pounding in large violent thumps. Time and again, sudden chills violently shook his entire body as if who knows what kind of storm raged inside him. Hot flashes shot up to his head and his eyes clouded over for a moment, so that Serpenera's body, at which he was stealthily staring, seemed gigantic. All of a sudden, Testagrossa's blood curdled, his whole body shook with fear. Serpenera was staring at him with an amazed, threatening expression. It seemed to say, 'What? Are you there?! So, will it take another stabbing?!'

For an instant, Testagrossa held the awful boy's gaze, then his eyes clouded over as if he were overcome by a strange sleepwalking state that made his blood run dry. The courage of that morning had been supplanted by a sense of strange fear. He felt that boy's eyes on him, wrapped all around him like a blanket of hot air that made him drowsy and sapped his will. He felt that if Serpenera had taken him by the hand, he would have let himself be pulled along anywhere, like a puppy. Maybe it was because he felt the frightening repulsion of being suffocated by a slimy hand that was still clenched around his neck.

He did not see anything in the show anymore. He did not hear anything anymore. His entire being struggled with that single thought – to escape from Serpenera. But how? The show could not go on forever, could it? In an hour they would have to go out into the small dark streets. Serpenera, Guercino, Manuzza, and the other hoodlums who surfaced all around as soon as night fell, like rats from the sewers, would hurl themselves on him.

Who should he ask for help?

Yes, inside this very theatre there were so many honest faces of labourers who would go straight home after the show, where their families were waiting for them. But these labourers were even more repelled by Serpenera and his companions than Testagrossa was. Not that they were afraid, because if necessary, they would have been good at breaking them all in two. But they wanted to avoid them because going to prison or to the hospital would not have been a solace for their mothers. The others instead, the petty thieves, had become hardened, and prison and the hospital were their habitual shelter. They stabbed people over nothing at all.

He could ask officer Troisi for help, the only man in the neighbourhood who knew how to keep that rabble submissive. But just the thought of resorting to the cop suddenly made his blood rise with an intense repugnance. So in order to escape Serpenera's persecution, Testagrossa had to find any means but that. But there was not any.

Meanwhile, looking furtively, he saw the awful boy's eyes still fixed on him. Serpenera suddenly leaned over and whispered something in Manuzza's ear. Manuzza stood up, turned, and looked straight at Testagrossa. So it concerned him. They were preparing his punishment. After a few minutes, Manuzza appeared in front of him. He had gone round the way, creeping along the wall. Testagrossa frowned, seeing him up close. The other guy impassively planted himself opposite him and guffawed, making his big mouth reach clear into his ears and spreading his nostrils, which were wide and mobile like a donkey's. He said, 'Oh! Testagrossa, what's the word?'

'He who has money lives happily,' answered Testagrossa, his teeth gnashing and voice faltering.

'But he who has no money, has friends.'

'I wouldn't know what to do with friends ... I'm alone and I want to stay alone.'

'That's bad. He who is alone has no good fortune.'

'It's better to have good friends or no friends at all ...'

'That's enough! Listen to what I'm telling you,' and Manuzza came right up close to him, his small eyes full of mocking laughter. 'Listen to what I'm telling you. You're the one who wants bad luck. Serpenera's waiting for you outside. We'll be in front of the door ... You won't be able to get away!'

Testagrossa just shrugged his shoulders in reply, but he grew livid and his chin started to tremble as if he were cold.

Manuzza went to stand next to the door. Serpenera and Guercino soon joined him. Serpenera stood in the middle, with one guy on his right and the other on his left. Testagrossa saw them and a chill of terrifying repulsion came over him again, because he felt the slimy grip of a filthy hand around his neck.

VII

On stage, there was a hell of an uproar, furious stomping accompanied the lightening-quick moves of two paladin combatants. There was a violent striking of swords on shields, helmets, and armour, and responding to each blow were shouts and a more frenzied fury in the blows and parries. Four paladins were present at the tremendous duel. All the spectators were on tenterhooks as they anxiously followed the skilful, violent blows delivered by the two paladins, who were full of an exceptional vitality that set the blood aflame with a vibrant throbbing of emulation. In that moment, all those young people had one single heroic heart that sent a gigantic strength through the muscles of their arms. At that point, each small spectator felt capable of the most daring undertaking ever. Not only that. Each of them also felt an unrestrainable desire to prove his own courage and his own strength, and to take some punches for no reason in the world. Following each shout of anger and incitement that accompanied an admirable strike of a sword, an unconscious, attenuated yell escaped from all the spectators, and their bodies suddenly stood up as if to attack some hidden enemy. All their fists were clenched, teeth and lips set, brows furrowed, eyes threatening. Each spectator imagined he was one of the two opposing warriors, and shook with rage at a blow received or thrilled with happiness at every blow well landed. Each one recalled to mind an enemy or formed an image of one, whoever it might be, on whom it would be fitting to let loose the storm of disdain, fury, and rage that screamed in his own heart. It was as if a furious wind were churning the spectators' little hearts. Even the barrel organ seemed caught up in an insane fury, the notes were so uproarious, crashing down like a cascade of cloudy, torrential water.

Testagrossa seemed changed too. The wave of heroism filling everyone's heart had dispelled his fear. He felt capable of facing Serpenera,

Manuzza, and Guercino, all three of them together, even armed with their knives.

All of a sudden, a terrible blow of the sword that a paladin delivers with both hands, striking the other's helmet, stuns his adversary, who staggers like a drunk. A muffled shout like the growl of angry wild animals echoes through the theatre. But Angelica, the fairest beauty Angelica, bursts on stage from the wings, and throws herself between the two combatants, interrupting the fight. A shout of disapproval follows the woman's act of pacification. But by then the curtain is slowly coming down, to the visible displeasure of all the spectators, who wanted one or the other of the tremendously strong paladins dead.

The shouting, smacking, nibbling of seeds, and gibes started up again. Here and there, where there was a bit of space, some of them tested their skills in little duels resembling those fought by the two paladins.

Testagrossa glanced towards the door. The three boys were staked out there, looking at him ferociously. Serpenera's look was threatening. But Testagrossa's fear was gone and he stared straight back at Serpenera so insistently that the other boy could not contain himself, and shouted a threat at him. Testagrossa replied with a snicker.

Furious, Serpenera was on top of the boy in a leap and a bound, and was about to punch him hard, but the young labourer, intervening in time, sent him tumbling between the benches with a violent smack in the face. Manuzza and Guercino, who had rushed over, and Serpenera, who had stood up with a roar, threw themselves on Testagrossa and the labourer, who held their own with hard punches and kicks, until some men intervened, separating them by dint of a few slaps.

'We'll see about this outside,' shouted Serpenera, while they dragged him towards the door.

'Yeah! I'll take away your taste for being a rotten bully for good!' yelled back the young labourer, sitting back down, calm and peaceful.

Testagrossa came to sit down next to him, and thanked him with an intense smile of affection.

'We'll leave together,' the labourer said to him, 'and you'll see, at the flash of the knife all three of them will run lightning fast, like *Barberi* horses.'

All the yelling, which had died down a bit because of the scuffle, had taken over the place again. But it promptly subsided, and entirely died out. What was going on?

It was officer Troisi coming in with four police agents from head-quarters. He was coming to perform one of the usual, frequent searches of the young men's pockets. But by then the visits were so well known and expected that none of the regular spectators would let themselves get caught red-handed. That only happened to someone who was just passing through the neighbourhood. The first people they searched were Serpenera, Manuzza, and Guercino.

Testagrossa looked all around. All the faces had turned dumb, their eyes nearly lifeless and lids lowered like pontificating saints. The young labourer was the only one whose face had turned red, his eyes staring and welled with tears. Testagrossa thought the boy was lost. He leaned over near his ear and whispered, 'Give it to me.' The labourer looked at him as if he were dreaming. He did not move, and the police agents were getting close. Testagrossa forcefully whispered, 'Fool, no one is waiting for me at home. Give it to me! From tomorrow on, I'll be eating three square meals a day.'

Then the other boy quickly stuck his hand in his pocket and passed the long knife to Testagrossa. When the police agent came up and found it in his pocket, all the faces were full of surprise. What? Was he such a fool? Didn't he expect Troisi's visit? When they took him away handcuffed like a thief, a murmur of disapproval followed him. But a sob followed him too, and perhaps a kiss that the young labourer sent him in his heart.

Outside, officer Troisi looked him straight in the eyes under the lamplight, and said, 'I wouldn't have believed it.' He handed him over to a police agent, who grabbed him by the wrist and made him trot along beside him all the way to the station, followed by a throng of speechless little scamps and the small labourer, who yelled to him only after the main door was shut, 'Oh, Testagrossa, take care, take care!'

But that was worse, because that voice took away the will power that had sustained him. It brought a lump to his throat and a flicker of tears on his lashes.

The entrance hall was full of darkness, a gloomy darkness broken only by the faint light cast by the lamp. The guard asked, 'Did he steal something?'

'No, he had a mean-looking knife.'

'He's off to a good start.'

'He didn't seem like it.'

'Is the inspector in?'

'He's in.'

In the small, narrow, low-ceilinged room, a little man sitting at a desk raised his head, which swayed back and forth as if his neck were broken. He wrinkled up his face, opened his little eyes just a crack, curled his upper lip, flared his nostrils as if to sniff the air, and said to the guard, 'Have him come in.'

The guard pushed Testagrossa up next to the desk and the inspector cast a sidelong glance at him, as if he were an exotic animal.

'I haven't seen you before. You're a new customer. But you've got a kilo of brains in that ugly dome of yours and, vice versa, you must have a heart as tiny as a peanut ... A bad sign.'

That unexpected reception made Testagrossa angry, and all the more so because he was going to jail at his own discretion. Biting words rose to his lips.

'A bad sign,' repeated the inspector, partly shutting his eyes and letting his small head sway back and forth, looking as if it might roll onto the desk at any moment. It seemed as if he were speaking in a dream. Testagrossa snapped, and blurted, 'I've never weighed them ...'

'What?' the inspector said, giving a start as if waking up again in that moment. He took a better look at Testagrossa and asked the guard, 'What did this rascal do?'

'My name's Testagrossa.'

It took all the inspector had to stifle his laughter, and he looked like a little monkey having a convulsion. The boy could barely keep himself from flying into a rage.

'He had this nasty knife on him,' said the guard.

The inspector put out a small white hand and drew the knife close to him, almost touching it with the tip of his nose. Then he said, 'Did you want to slit someone's throat?'

'I didn't want to slit anyone's throat.'

'Shut up! Don't do that again!'

'But if you ask me something ...'

'Quiet, little scoundrel.'

Testagrossa stomped his feet and bit his lips, because the way he was being treated revolted him. But on the sly, the guard kicked him in the leg. Then Testagrossa stomped his feet harder, and got the guard, who gave him a hard slap. Testagrossa jumped back and in a few leaps was at the door. But the door was closed and the guard came to grab him. It was a short fight. Testagrossa struggled, hitting and kicking like a madman. Some other guards rushed up at all the noise, tied his hands

up tight behind his back, slapped him, and took him back in front of
the inspector.

'I told you so. That ugly dome is a bad sign. And there's a snub nose
and big mouth too. What's your name?'

'Testagrossa's my name.'

'That's a nickname.'

'That's what they call me. I don't know anything else.'

'Your father?'

'My father? What do I know. I don't remember. They called him
Lupo Mannaro, Wolf-man.'

The inspector jumped, as if he'd been bitten by a snake. 'Ah! So then,
your father was Lupo Mannaro. Listen to this, guards! Listen! Just like
his father, this wolf cub. Do all of you remember, in this very room?
Lupo Mannaro, years ago ... How many of you others were wounded?
We had to crack that devil's head open to subdue him. It was only after
he lost a lot of blood that he finally quieted down!

'And now you want to start too. You want to show your claws rather
early. But we'll clip them off, clear down to the roots.'

Testagrossa did not understand a thing. Before his eyes was a cloudy
vision of his father struggling amidst a crowd of police agents. It was
as if he saw him squatting down in that dark corner of the small room,
panting heavily in deep breaths. But beyond the dark room, out in the
open sunshine, he saw a fair woman with a sweet face. He got a lump
in his throat that he drove back down with a small roar, but he could
not drive back the big tears streaming down his cheeks. The inspector
saw the tears glistening in the lamplight, and said:

'Tears of anger, huh? But there's nothing you can do about it. Who
knows how many more tears you'll shed locked up in the coop! Until
you get your calluses. For now, we'll send you to San Martino, to the
youth camp. There are lots of good boys like you there. Small-time
career thieves, stabbers, and the sons of "famous men." You'll find the
brigand Varsalona's son there. Fortunately, that one doesn't take after
his father. He's the best boy in the youth camp. A miracle! Who knows!
But you'll make it a career, you'll see.'

Testagrossa did not hear anything the inspector was mumbling on
about while he wrote up the police report. He was concentrating on
holding back the wave of tears welling up and the cries of anguish,
'What had she done? What had she done?'

When the inspector had written up the report, he turned to the guards and concluded, 'Lock him up. But keep an eye on him. Remember, he's Lupo Mannaro's cub.'

The guard led Testagrossa out by the collar of his jacket, with his hands tied behind his back. Testagrossa crossed the shadowy courtyard. Two guards were dozing on the bench. Hearing the shuffling footsteps they stood up. One of them got the keys, which jangled loudly, and the other one brought the lantern, which cast splashes of blood-red light on the black cobblestones. They reached the prison door. There was the screech of the key opening the lock. The two guards went in first. A wave of horrid stench, of rats' nests and thick heat, came from the closed space. Here and there, the reddish light cut through the gloomy darkness. The shape of a big body crouching on a bench and snoring loudly appeared. Testagrossa recoiled, overcome by repulsion. But the guard gave him a big push that sent him tumbling into a corner.

'Lie down there ...'

It turned pitch-dark again. The key turning in the lock screeched, then the tread of footsteps became fainter and fainter. The snoring stopped, a deep silence descended.

Testagrossa crumbled in the corner where he had fallen, leaning his head against the wall, and painfully strained his ears, as if to grab onto any sound at all that might give a sign of life. And then from far away, like a faint voice of memory, the echo of singing reached him. Testagrossa got up on his knees and stretched his neck. It was tearful singing, calling for someone. The boy had heard such intensely painful singing once before, perhaps. The last note hung trembling in the air, then it died out. And the darkness all around became blacker.

The boy was overcome by an inconsolable weakness, by a mortal impotence, as if all his blood had drained from his open veins. His heart was drowned in a never-ending sea of pain. He started to cry then, as if he were one of those children who have a mama, as if by crying inconsolably two merciful hands might come to gather him up. It was a sorrowful crying, broken at regular intervals by a slow, full lament, like a dirge.

All of a sudden, Testagrossa clenched his teeth and shook his head, as if to summon the strength of will that had abandoned him, because he heard the big body move, then a groping on the planks and a measured shuffling. Someone, maybe the man who had been snoring, was coming over to him.

In fact, feeling a warm, stinking breath on his face, Testagrossa moved back. But a mild voice mumbled, 'What are you doing? Crying? Who are you? What's your name? Say something.'

'My name's Testagrossa.'

'I don't know you. Are you from this neighbourhood?'

'Yes.'

'Speak softly. But I don't know you. What did you do?'

Testagrossa told him everything, from the time they arrested him to his attempt to escape.

'Who was there?'

'The inspector and the guards.'

'It's nothing then. But you need a mafioso lawyer. Who's defending you?'

'Me? No one.'

'Your father?'

'He's dead.'

'Well then, who do you know?'

'Me? I don't know anyone.'

'You're a bird just learning to fly. But you spread your wings well. With a little teaching you'll fly far, as the light is true. What was your father's name?'

'His name was Lupo-Mannaro!'

'Ah! Ah! You come from good stock. Listen, do you want to get out fast? Let me take care of it. Do you know Manuzza?'

'Yes.'

'And Serpenera?'

'Him too.'

'But aren't you friends?'

'No.'

'Well, listen. Serpenera and Manuzza come in here often. But they also get out often, because the lawyer defends them. And then, I talk to the people accusing them of something. And right away, they say, 'Inspector, go on! It's not true. None of it! Serpenera and Manuzza are good boys.' If you get out of here soon, just think how furious the inspector and the police will be! If not, they'll keep you at San Martino till you're twenty. Up there, on the mountain, shut up inside four walls. Water, bread, and a few lashes to go with it. And you'll work like a mule.'

'And what do I have to do?'

'What do you have to do? Nothing. You have to be our good friend. Become Serpenera's pal, and help him sometimes. Just when it's needed. You can count on them being the best relatives of all. But if you get on better staying with the cops ...'

'Better to die!' exclaimed Testagrossa, feeling the furious hate boil up inside him again. What had he done? Why had they treated him like a dog? And he added firmly, 'Yes, I want to be with you.'

'Good. I'll be out in a little while. I'll see Serpenera. What should I tell him?'

'Tell him Testagrossa agrees.'

'My dear boy! You see, you're good at reckoning up sums. Your father, God rest him, is illuminating your mind. Don't say anything. As if I never said a word to you. You're a man. Mind you! Always silent as a grave.'

'Do you know who I am? I'm Don Lucio, Serpenera's boss.'

The big body moved away, groping along, got on the bench again, and immediately there was a noisy snoring, as if the man were already in a deep sleep. A hurried shuffling came from outside, then the key screeched and a strip of red light cut through the darkness. Two guards came in.

'Don Lucio, Don Lucio,' said one of the guards, shaking the man. But he was busy snoring.

'Don Lucio, Don Lucio ... Are you having a really good sleep?'

They heard a deep sigh, then a big 'Ah!' The man stretched his arms, rubbed his eyes, and as if completely amazed, said 'Eeks! Where am I? Merciful Virgin Mary!' He rubbed his eyes again. Then, while he dusted himself off and straightened his suit, he said, 'Gosh, I didn't remember anymore! I was dreaming, see. I was dreaming I was sitting at the table having lunch. My wife was here, my children over there. Four children, you know. But really beautiful, like four shining stars. And my godfather was there too. A real gentleman. In fact, my godfather was drinking to my family's health. When I hear "Don Lucio, Don Lucio" and then the shaking ... It was you waking me up. I was sleeping the sleep of the just. Yes, I certainly was.'

The guards smiled as if to say, 'Hey, friend, you know what's what. Thank God that you have a lot of people protecting you. But if you slip up, you'll pay for everything all at once.'

'The inspector has given the order for your release,' said the guard.

'May God reward the person who looked after me.'

The guards went out first, and as Don Lucio passed by, he touched Testagrossa with his foot. As if still carrying on the conversation, he said loudly, 'He who has faithful friends can sleep without worry.'

Testagrossa understood for sure that those words were meant for him, and he felt a shiver run through him. It was over! There were *friends* who were looking after him, now that he was sending someone to tell Serpenera, '*Testagrossa agrees!*'

NOTES

1　*Testagrossa* means, literally, big head. The description of the character's large head and tiny body suggests he suffers from malnutrition.
2　*Zia*, literally 'aunt' or 'auntie,' was a popular expression used by young people to address middle-aged people.
3　Florio, who organized the first automobile races, was among the most wealthy Sicilians of the time.
4　*Muffutu* is the dialect expression for spy.
5　Orlando is a famous paladin in the marionette performances of the Opera dei Pupi, one of the art forms for which Sicily is renowned.
6　The white coins were made of silver, the black ones of copper.
7　Rodomonte is another figure in the Sicilian puppet theatre, known as an aggressive, bragging warrior.
8　A popular expression for being beaten up.
9　Military sharpshooters.
10　The rank of a brigadiere in the carabinieri is similar to that of sergeant in the army.

The Hired Killer

GRAZIA DELEDDA

No one, among the people who knew about his terrible profession and more or less made use of him or counted on making use of him, called him by this name. Indeed, everyone thought of him, at least superficially, as an executioner. Because, in fact, he would not lend himself to the requested *executions* unless the cases were exceptional, that is, when it was a matter of a just vendetta or getting rid of an individual who was harming the peace of a man or family. He always studied the *case* in detail if not in depth, before coming to an irrevocable decision, without any high scruples, without any religious principles, without any superstitions. He did not believe in God, or a life hereafter. He did not believe in official justice. In fact, his first execution had been on his own account, after losing a lawsuit that had gone from small to big, and from civil court had ended up in the supreme court, and ruined him. And he had been in the right. His home was put up for auction, his furniture sold. He gnashed his teeth with rage, and the pain of the injustice. His blood ran calm only when he finally saw the blood of his persecutor.

When he became a killer, the judicial authority did not punish him or even search for him. So he harboured an almost ironic, if not cynical, sense of the freedom that a man has to take the law into his own hands. One evening during the early times of poverty and dejection, drunk with wine and bitterness, he had spoken about his firm belief to a friend who was complaining about how he in turn was being persecuted and threatened with ruin and death by an adversary of his.

'Get rid of him! There's nothing else to do.'

But his friend was a weak, fearful person, and said so, adding, however, that if he found someone willing to help him he would not be sorry.

The drunken man asked, 'How much are you offering?'

They looked each other in the eyes the way demons must look at each other.

Now, after many years and successful results, a special case presented itself. The man, who had rebuilt a fortune and often travelled dealing in horses, arrived one day at the home of a widow, still young and of a devastating, arrogant beauty. Her house rose in the middle of a bluish cloud of olive groves halfway up the mountain, atop of which the little grey town seemed to spring from the very stone. She was so rich that while the men in the area rode donkeys, she had horses to sell.

They went to see them in the sloping meadow of green, which turned nearly black in the shadow of the mountain soaring above, where the horses grazed, white, solid, with hard lines, as if rough-hewn from marble. In fact, they were solid work horses, and after looking in their mouths and feeling every bit of their bodies, the man was satisfied.

Back inside the house after the contract was settled, the woman offered him something to drink – a strong, fragrant wine that the man, though a drinker, had not tasted before. Perhaps this was why his blood went immediately aflame. In fact, it was the woman's presence and manner that excited him, since she looked at him in a strange way with her big black and yellow eyes, tempestuous, not alluring. Indeed, it was as if they were animated by a light of hate and distrust.

Since he was talking in a good-natured, friendly manner, it was she who explained the reason right away.

'You bear an extraordinary resemblance to a person I know. You may know him too. The miller down at the steam oil mill. Are you related, perhaps?'

'I've never seen him, never met him, never heard his name,' the man answered, with light irony. 'And you?'

'Me? Unfortunately, I've made his acquaintance. He's swindled me a thousand different ways.'

'This doesn't flatter my resemblance. I hope you're not giving me these furtive looks because you're afraid my heart resembles him too.'

'Right, right,' she said laughing, reassured. 'Your eyes are different. They're the eyes of an honest man.'

He did not lower his eyes, because with her he felt not only like an honest man, but, at least for the moment, a generous friend too.

Then she began to tell him about the miller's swindles, which, according to the law, were not even swindles because she had lent him money without any interest or promissory notes. And he had no thought of paying it back.

'Last winter, he even kept the oil from my olives, with the promise that he would sell it at a good price. And he did sell it, damn him, for his own profit.'

'But, please forgive me for an indiscrete question. Don't you have any men, relatives I mean, with the guts to make everyone respect you?'

'I don't have anyone. I'm not from this town. I have some relatives on my poor husband's side. But those old crows – they live up in town. They hate me because my late husband left me all of his property. They're the first to rejoice when some misfortune comes my way.'

The man sipped his wine and turned pensive. His old executioner instinct reawakened, but in a noble form, almost tender.

'But what pretext did this friend use?'

'Oh, it's a long story,' she said, with a vague gesture. 'I'll tell you about it another time, if we see each other again.'

They saw each other again, because he found a lot of excuses for going back to her house. She received him sullenly. She became all the more sullen and distrustful the more friendly and unselfish he acted. Although he kept returning to the subject of the miller, she did not tell the long story she had promised. But he had already guessed. One day he just said, 'I finally met my double. He's boasting about some nice little stories, about you.'

She sprang up tall and outstretched, her hands like claws, looking as if she would pounce on the man to scratch him, while he laughed and opened his arms as if to gather her in them and console her.

Then she bent down in front of the fire in the fireplace, took a red-hot ember and drew a fiery cross on the floor. She said hoarsely, 'No one knew what he really was to me. But since he's bragging about it now, I swear to God I'll set fire to his house.'

'Calm down, come on,' said the man, disarming her of the ember. 'Now we're going to talk. Give me something to drink.'

Agitated, she went to get the wine. They sat next to the fire since the weather was already cold, and she told the long story about love, betrayal, and robbery.

'He took advantage of me because I'm a woman all alone, defenceless. At the end, after he'd squeezed me like a lemon, he said sure, he would keep his promise of marriage. But on the condition I give him everything that's mine. That's how far this murderer went. But now it's my turn.'

The man stood up, put his glass on the table, and sat down again, moving his chair up close to hers. He felt all warm with generosity. He liked the woman for that very hate of hers, for the passion that gushed more from her gestures and terrible eyes than her words. And also because she did not complain, she did not ask for help, but intended to avenge herself on her own. Drawing his face close to hers, he whispered, 'If I did something for you, would you be happy?'

She gave a start. She looked him in the eyes, and he remembered the eyes of the first person who had hired him to kill.

That same day he explored the area around the oil mill for the first time. It was a simple black building, whose walls almost oozed oil. The oil press was rumbling from inside as it crushed the olives. A large wisp of smoke billowed from the smokestack and the oily black rivulet of dregs flowed out of a hole beside the door. Everything was depressing around the barren crags and the slope beneath the building, scattered with volcanic rocks. One almost felt as if the man roosted in there with his trade could not be a man of good feelings.

Even the peasants, lean and dark, with their long, drooping mustaches, who came downhill with their donkeys loaded with sacks of olives, had a grotesque, sinister look. Or was it the horse dealer who saw things like that, everything ugly because his thoughts were ugly?

After all, he was not *convinced* this time. He felt as if he were driven by some kind of fate. Far away from the woman's presence and the sensual charm she wielded over him, his irrational hate for the oil miller dissolved.

In any case, out of curiosity he was determined to actually meet his double. He did not need an excuse; he wanted to buy a barrel of olive oil. So he went inside, where the oil press was, and asked for the owner. He felt a sense of joy when an old man looking after the machine replied that the owner was ill. He immediately asked about his illness.

'Who knows! He went up to town the other day and says he drank a glass of wine with a stranger to these parts. When he got back here he started to have pains and throw up. He thinks he was poisoned. But today he feels better.'

'May I see him?'

They let the man see him. He was in his clothes lying on a small bed in a room jammed with jugs of oil and baskets of green olives. He had wound a rosary around his wrist, and a small votive light burned in front of a little statue of the Madonna on a small table beside him.

The horse dealer did not even see the striking resemblance the widow claimed was there. Perhaps because of his illness and unshaven beard shadowing his cheeks, the miller looked older than him, with cold, light-coloured eyes, almost the colour of the olives around him. Through the window you could see a whitish, rocky landscape in the cold sunset, which looked as if it were drawn with chalk on a chalkboard. The horse dealer must have remembered all of this as the gloomiest picture he had ever seen in his life.

He stood there for just a few minutes, and exchanged just a few words with the sick miller. Then he went away with a free heart, because after experiencing a mysterious sensation of fear for the first time in his life, almost as if he had penetrated an inhuman place where the worst monsters of fate reigned invisibly, he had decided not to get mixed up any further in the widow's affairs.

Three days later he was arrested. The miller had died, poisoned in fact, yelling in his final hours of delirium that the outsider he had had a drink with up in town was the same one who came to make a deal for a barrel of oil.

In vain did the horse dealer give proof to the contrary. Unconscious, the justice of men had driven him down the path of crime, and unconscious, it punished him for the only crime he had not committed.

The Carob Tree

MARIA OCCHIPINTI

In the peasant neighbourhood, behind Teresa's house, there was an abandoned meadow with a big carob tree. The young people used to go there often, preparing a banquet-style meal to eat all together in the shade. They spent their days making clothes and caps out of the carob leaves, patiently weaving them together with the stems. They cooked dried legumes in a big old pot. The little boys amused themselves gathering heaps of firewood, and the little girls fed the fire down on their knees, blowing on the embers. The flame leaped and the smoke spread around the tree.

The mothers would sit in front of the weaver's door. Some women would knit, some worked at their Sicilian stitch[1] embroidery, and others cleaned the dried legumes or wheat. A few women would spin yarn or thread. They always talked about the same things, hoping it would not rain because then their husbands would not lose a day's work. All the women shared the same poverty. At midday, they ate their lunch together. Each of the women had a piece of bread with some tomato, some celery, or onion in her apron, a few had a salted sardine. Some of them would offer prickly pears grown on their land. They ate hungrily, and drank from the same pitcher, taking turns. Now and then one of the small children ran up from the meadow to ask his mama for some bread, and she modestly took it from her breast, giving the child a little piece. The weaver sang the usual song so her baby boy in the swinging cot would not cry:

Quiet my boy
for now I'll hold you
I'll give you my breast
for there is no bread

And between one shuttle and the next, she pulled the cord hanging from the cot, which she kept tied to the loom.

Teresa's mother served as a nurse when there was a baby to deliver or a cut to make. Then there was Ugo, the son of the captain of the black shirts, who would go to the meadow to play with Teresa. And there was Saru, a thin boy with dark skin like a little African, bright eyes, and a heart of gold. He stole bread from home and hid it in the cat holes so he could give it to the famished dogs later. One day he brought back a pregnant dog. So they built a hut out of old sacks under the carob tree, to protect her from the cold at night. Saru sat close beside her until late into the night.

Toward sunset, the mothers called their children, who ran home to eat their soup of cabbage and legumes. But Saru did not feel the need to go home, tired from the long trips to the river where he caught crabs and frogs with Neli, one of the crop broker's children, who was good at hunting birds with a slingshot. After vainly shouting herself hoarse, Saru's mother, who knew how her son was, went to get him in the meadow, and promised him some bread and soup for the dog. So they put some of the dish-watery soup with bits of bread in an old bowl. Saru often ate his soup with dirty hands and uncombed hair. He did not pay any mind to school or the homework he was supposed to do for the next day. The old schoolbag sat on a small chair under the table. His problem was to take care of the dog. He would run to take her the warm broth, and the crop broker's children, who ate on their front steps, would give him some spoonfuls of their food when he passed by. Ugo brought little chicken bones, and Franco, the blacksmith's son, brought fish heads.

When it got dark, everyone gathered in the middle of the street for the theatre performance. They impatiently waited for Turi. He worked as an errand-boy in the baron's home. After he had finished his chores and washed the stairs, he played with the baron's son who, though younger than Turi, taught him all about the battle of Rizziero and Fioravanti. They also waited for Nané to leave the movie theatre, where he sold candies. Once everyone was there, they started to perform. They had daggers made out of wood and fake beards. Nané was really great at leading the fighters! Turi wore bronze sabres that his boss's son had given him. Giovanni, whose father was a political refugee in America, was there too. He played the part of the wild giant. This way they also attracted the adults' curiosity. You saw people killed, wounded, defeated. Their fury was so great that the entire neighbourhood rushed over to watch. Among the people watching the show, there were some who even stood on chairs to get a better view of the warriors.

Saru was not part of that world for he always stayed close to the dog, sleeping right next to her, and oftentimes his father would carry him home in his arms. One beautiful morning, Saru discovered the dog with six puppies around her. Everyone heard the screams of joy, and soon a small crowd of little children and women went to see the dog. Everyone was touched by the event. The mother dog turned fierce if anyone went near. Only Saru could get close to her, pick up the puppies and show them to everyone. Saru thought he needed to get some warm milk, and bands of wool to cover the puppies, but nobody had any money for the milk. The small children drank milk only when they were sick. Saru went to Ugo's house looking for some money, and the boy gave it to him. Saru's mother warmed the milk while all the children gathered around the mother dog, their eyes full of envy as they watched her drink the milk, but at the same time full of hope too, because they wanted to have one of the puppies for themselves. His father had to intervene to divide them up.

That abandoned meadow and that carob tree were paradise for the neighbourhood children. On Sundays, when they went to Sunday school, their mothers went on the swing up in the tree, and dug a shallow basin in the dirt to play the hazel-nut game.[2] With the beautiful days, they spent their Sundays like this in the meadow. This chorus of women was also able to bring their husbands together in a sort of brotherly way. They were like a family. They shared the same poverty and the same hope, they comforted one another and helped each other out as best they could. There was never a quarrel, they had all known each other since childhood, they all had their little house that they owned. When daughters married, they stayed in their father's home at first, but with time, by saving up, they managed to build a home for themselves next door to her parents. An old disabled man and a blind man lived in the neighbourhood. They would tell stories, and everybody listened, paying close attention. Then there was one woman who was wiser, and gave advice on clothes, on the quality of things that last, on marriages. As a matchmaker, she knew if a certain girl could be suited for a certain boy or not. She arranged marriages without the girls knowing anything about it, relying blindly on what the parents wanted. So the days went by among that band of people who thought of everyone as relatives.

Later on, a family who had been in America came to live in the neighbourhood. People said the father had been part of the 'black hand,' and had repatriated to escape from the police. He had three children: a boy, who played the violin and was good at drawing portraits in pencil, and two girls, one who was studying to be a teacher and the little one who went to embroidery school.

This man worked in the office at the local Fascist Party headquarters. The peasant women knew he was a thief and did not trust him hardly at all. To be polite, they paid him a visit when someone in his family was ill, and when they went inside his home they felt a kind of embarrassment. The house was tastefully furnished, differently than their own homes, where everything was austere: two rooms at the most, one with a large crucifix hanging over the double bed, a few votive lights on the chest of drawers, lit for Saint Joseph and Saint Anthony, the chairs standing around, and the table, with the water pitcher in the middle. The other room was divided in two, with the donkey on one side (you smelled the stink of manure from a distance) and the children's bed on the other, with starched white pillowcases on the pillows, soon soiled by the flies.

The thief's house was not like that. It was on the second floor. The stairway was covered in black pitch that shined like marble, the rooms were airy, the tiles on the floor were in beautiful colours, paintings full of landscapes were hung on the wall, easy chairs at the foot of the bed. There was a beautiful velvet cover on the table, with a beautiful bouquet on top, along with some books and a dictionary. None of the peasants knew what a dictionary was.

When this family sat out on the balcony, the son drew sketches, the little girl embroidered, and the mother read. Before that, no one had seen a woman reading a book. Their home had a different scent to it, not the scent of pomegranates and quinces, or of lavender or jasmine, and without the stink of the donkey and chickens. It was beautiful because it did not have these smells. The peasant women forbade their children to associate with these children because their father was being followed by the cops, and because of him the police scoured the neighbourhood. Seeing these unfamiliar faces, they sighed with regret, saying the neighbourhood used to be an abbey before, and now it was under surveillance. They had lost peace and unity, the women had become selfish. Each of them thought only of herself, and concealed the slightest thing as if their homes were full of mysteries. It was not like that before, when a neighbour woman's sorrow was everyone's sorrow, as was her joy. Luxury and haughtiness were born. Everyone felt like bigwigs. These were the peasants' complaints. The working-class man sent his children to the dances, husbands caressed their wives in front of their children. You never saw that before, people were more serious. A wife and husband addressed each other with formality. The workmen's wives were more brazen; they did not have a lot of children.

Teresa saw it as a wonderful world. Even Iolanda's father, though he had the reputation of being a thief, seemed like a marquis. He dressed well, was respectful with the neighbour women, and very loving with his children, hugging and kissing them, even out on the balcony. Everyone saw and criticized it, convinced that children should be kissed only when they are sleeping.

In the peasant world, the father had to be respected and, most of all, feared, and therefore, relations were strict. Teresa wanted an affectionate father, like a friend to whom she could confide what was in her heart, and a loving mother. The peasant women were strict, the mother was never a friend, and what woes if there were differences between their ideas and tastes. The mother wielded threats, and the daughter could not confide the secret that she was engaged on the sly, or there would have been a thrashing and the father could have killed her. Children feared parents like a thief fears the law. The mother, so as not to disobey her husband and not lose peace in the family, was the harshest tyrant of all over the daughter.

In Iolanda's home, there was harmony, love. The thief-man, whom everyone in the neighbourhood singled out as the monster to be afraid of, was instead a perfect father of the family. Teresa believed thieves had a fierce face, she imagined them as monsters with a knife between their teeth, who 'steal the little livers out of children.' As her grandmother used to say, 'Don't go out at night, because the thief steals children and tears out their little livers.' Now the thief was not that terrible monster in the story, but a wonderful symbol. Teresa could not understand the fear and disdain people bore towards him.

One Sunday morning, while everyone was returning from church, they saw Iolanda's father pass by in handcuffs, walking between four cops. The man's face was pale as wax, his head bent so as not to meet the eyes of the neighbour women, who saw him and drew back, exclaiming, 'Neither shock nor surprise!' to keep away a similar destiny.

In Sicily some people believe that each person has a stone to carry, whether in prison or the hospital, so people never know what might happen to them. Teresa's mother, crossing herself, said, 'So this is the good man, may God save us, he's a thief! The other night they broke into a bank. That's why his children are dressed like bigwigs. Your father, who works like a dog, can't afford the luxury of having a new suit. We had to dye the one from two years ago to make it look decent. You wear inexpensive shoes on Sundays, and the cobbled-up ones the rest of the week. Instead, they're dressed up in party clothes. Truth will out!'

Every Sunday, while the other families ate in peace, Iolanda would leave with a bag to take her father food to eat in prison. She and her sister passed by with heads bowed, and the neighbour women had pity on them.

NOTES

1 Embroidery in the Sicilian stitch (*il cinquecento*) is a beautiful, complex art. Material is placed on a frame and threads are pulled out. The empty spaces are then filled back in with often intricate embroidery designs, angels being a frequent motif. I thank Lilia Milli for this information.
2 What Occhipinti calls the 'hazel-nut game' has several variations. In general, a triangle is formed with three nuts, and to win the game the players take turns tossing a nut to make the top one fall.

Montelepre

ANNA MARIA ORTESE

After a lazy, boring Sunday, a photographer and I left Palermo again on Monday morning, February 7th, believing we would simply venture into places where banditry was famous. For us, Montelepre was one of the many romantic itineraries in Sicily, a land of beautiful, all too isolated people. This seductive and morally pleasing conviction, which dissipated any suspicion of slightly more profound facts, accompanied us as far as the suburbs on the outskirts of Palermo – to those new houses, those old streets, the peach trees that continue the tradition of a blissful Sicily, despite everything, where the soil is continually vitalized by the warm breath of Africa, and nature lavishes comforting beauty on human solitude.

And then suddenly, as happens now and then in some resplendent dream, everything calmly began to turn dark. Even though we avidly looked all around, we could not see any shape that might remind us of nature and humankind – not a tree, not a hill, not a cart or a solitary wheel. Nor did we hear a voice, or the sound of footsteps or some instrument or object produced by human hands. We saw no light, though we could not say for sure if it were nighttime. A sort of twilight, fixed at the point where everything that exists continually seems to vanish and return, and then disappear again, was the fluid matter in which some blind, large, inert thing emerged and seemed to meet us for the first time. This thing – it hardly makes sense to name it – was stone.

Though we looked every which way, there was nothing but stone. To say that this stone had any sort of appearance could mean expressing the hope that this presence might have limits, might come to an end, because there are things that are impossible to tolerate for more than a flash. But that stone, the enormity and frightful indomitability of the stone, from which, as if from inside a womb, it was impossible to perceive anything, did not display any features. At the most, thinking about it, it perhaps was a womb, one cavity followed by other cavities in the middle of which arose some crests, some humps, and everything was preceded, followed, sustained, covered, surrounded by a tempest of curves, concentric circles, quarries, and manifold spirals of stone. Ages ago, before the world blossomed, this area must have been liquid too, and a storm of stone now marked the impassible place where scorching clouds rushed headlong, piled up, then deflated and expired in a sound that went beyond anything ever heard and any memory of humankind. Or meteors rained down upon it. But in contrast to other regions of the world, here the process of solidification happened suddenly, arresting that world in its fury. Nor did other processes follow to limit its horror. Everything was precisely as it was 'in those days.'

There are moments when a person trembles from head to toe, and the only thought that comes and goes in our mind with no other real consistency is how we will get through the next moment. It seems insurmountable, like a mountain made of crystal with perpendicular sides, and our anguish lies at the foot of this mountain. Our astonishment, however, comes to our aid. It is born from the same enormity of fear, from all that deafness and opacity that go along with delirious, dreadful perceptions and make it possible to register it. While the mind vacillates, astonishment softens its slips. We would say to each other, 'This stone has no shape, but it's huge.' By thinking this, we could get through the next moment.

At times we would even have liked to scream, just as in a dream, but we never could. We would have liked to drink something strong, a white river on which to cast off our fear, towards any outlet, but we had nothing of that sort in the car. All the wonders of the cafes were so very close, a few kilometres away, yet still extremely distant. We had gone back in time, these were the days of stone – the melancholy, nighttime, ambush, fury, and infinite weakness of the stone.

Sitting in front of us, the man driving had an ironic smile. We saw it in the rear-view mirror, but perhaps it was not even ironic: two dark eyes, glazed and staring ahead, the same eyes one sees on trains at dawn. The irony stemmed from detachment, a sort of solemn calm, sympathy, and harshness with which he viewed those things. As if he were cold, he was bundled up in a tattered coat, too tight and too short for his build, and hunched over the steering wheel, like a wounded man. Thick black hair, a real mane, escaped from an extremely small cyclist cap and rained down on his slender neck, brushing the collar of his coat. He was about thirty, and beneath his destroyed appearance there was still tenacity and resistance, and grace – the same grace with which small, intelligent individuals surrounded by brutal forces grant themselves a dignified death.

Still looking steadily straight ahead, he said, 'The mountain has eaten men, and has also drunk. It shows it was hungry and thirsty.'

But he said it calmly, with a kind of nonchalance, using the gentle voice of men of spirit faced with enormous, stupid things destined to defeat them.

The mountain had eaten men, and had also drunk. We understood two things all at once. This terrible matter, this infinite stone in which we had advanced to the point of losing sight of everything that might have colour and shape, was still the world, although there was no movement or the slightest glimmer of it, it was the world. Far from nourishing men, here nature watched their steps to draw them to her breast and consume them in her impassive embrace. Her hands, forehead, eyes were stone. Her voice, womb, milk were stone. And to be sure, the men were made of stone, though their spirit still belonged to God. Made of stone, and constantly in the act of defending themselves from their mother: vigilant, distrustful, pitiless, and remorseless each and every time. Worried for no reason, cheerful in their blood alone, distracted in the hours of repose, nearly always devoid of language, meditative, calm, unhappy.

We did not see them (there was not any sign of a human being on this land), but we started to sense them. Perhaps it was the wind's breath suddenly coming towards us from the mouths of certain gorges. Or certain rocks, larger than usual, that looked like the knees of men sitting. Or certain rare glimmers in the sky, imitating remote, bright eyes. The very sound of our car was the panting of someone groping about alone in a ditch, trying to come into the light.

Meanwhile, a veil might have fallen from our eyes or our car might have emerged from some tremendous lowland that had seemed interminable due to our slow speed, for what we had defined as formless was not so any more. The stone continued to surround us on all sides like a sea, but it had clear, precise contours. It was a continual flight of small bald mountains, one identical to the other, barely differing in size; barren, uninhabited, peaceful valleys; gorges through which you caught a glimpse of other smaller mountains with flat, bare summits and bare valleys with something alive running through them, like a shiver that moved around, constantly illuminating or extinguishing them. When it animated them certain white goats, or a deep black bull appeared, as if in a dream, and when it extinguished them, the bull and the goats were not there anymore. Growing melancholic, we looked up high above and saw that the extinguishing or animating of those small valleys was determined by large fog banks passing by fast and silent in the sky, coming from the area where we were headed. A thousand whitish puffs of smoke, turbid, almost fluid, were galloping galloping soundlessly among those grey mountaintops, like an enormous lost herd, like delicate livestock in flight from a place where something horrible was happening, like large animals from a burned-out town, staggering and worn out, that start to arrive and soon the surrounding plains are full of them, and the carcasses of the dead are suddenly submerged by the confused fury of new herds. Then, finally, there is nothing but a throb and absolute pain. This was exactly how those puffs of fog were chasing each other and piling up on top of one another, leaving the flat or round mountaintops all alone, or veiling them for just a moment, while the mass sank into the valleys.

That spectacle, incredible for a town of the south, confirmed our first sinister impression. This land was a million years behind in the history of the world, where everything was still in the initial stage, and every phenomenon seemed possible, every promise appeared probable, and from the stones to the atmosphere above everything was still waiting for definition.

This is what we were thinking, but very vaguely, because the intensity of every sensation pressed against our foreheads and prevented us from reflecting, when something, a whitish blotch with lots of eyes, appeared at the top of a hill, spun around, and vanished.

We saw it again a moment later, just when the man driving re-emerged from his remote silence and informed us in the same gentle, slightly despairing voice he had used before, 'From here they were shooting like madmen, "*isso*" ['*isso*' = it or he, in this case *he* – 'Giuliano'] and the carabinieri. This is the Bellolampo barracks.'

Surrounded by a little fence, it was a small, two-storey house, maybe pink, maybe white. We saw it very clearly now because the car had stopped in front of the gate. A man, a young man in shirtsleeves, was sitting on a rock cleaning a pipe with a knife. Another man, also in shirtsleeves, was standing further off with one arm raised, his hand leaning against the wall of the house. He was blond, with a wide face and calm eyes, full of the same expression, drowsy and watchful, not good, but at the same time not evil either – just hard and sad – that we had seen in the infinite photographs of *isso*. He watched us arrive without moving away from the wall; he did not move his head an inch, or raise an eyelid, as if we were not real, but the fruit of his imagination. Or else, as if any movement or thought seemed useless. The young man cleaning the pipe with the knife did not waste any time on looking at us either. Another man who was at the window on the first floor, his arms resting on the windowsill, his face set in the crook of his crossed arms like a woman, brushed his long blond curls slightly off his forehead and looked at us, but, we were convinced, without really seeing us.

Those men, who unquestionably belonged to the forces of the law, were there (and we will never know how much of this impression was subjective, an illusion, and how much was real) as in a dream bubble, with no colour, breath, or movement that might signal some sort of reality. It was as if time, solitude, memories had drained them of blood and desires. They were no more alive than the stones on which they rested their arms, their feet, no more substantial than the banks of fog that were chased by a light wind and flew silently over the small house. Behind the front of the house, on both the right and the left, the desert, that grey wave of stone, that immobile uniformity, continued. No, no word exists that can express the desperation of all this. But upon reflection, it was above all the uniformity and impassibility of everything, the calm full of the eternal in which this stone was lost, that suggested the sense of castigation, an immense life of imprisonment in which the men of the law had also ended up forever.

The driver rolled down the car window and yelled a greeting, but no one replied. Maybe they did not hear him. Maybe they heard, but for some reason unknown to us, no one thought it was good to reply.

The car started off again, and now some small forts return to mind. We do not know if they appeared before or after Bellolampo. Probably after, if the sight of them did not convey a stronger emotion, but left us calm, like seeing something vaguely familiar. They looked like large cattle heads, bare skulls abandoned along the road. Very very white, with two deep holes like eyes. There were no pupils, yet they had a look full of passionate memory, and they followed us. There too, surely, men had fired shots, and the hissing and screams had echoed through the rocks.

Another uphill slope began. By now we were not looking at any-thing anymore, we were cold and felt a faceless fear, like pneumonia with no fever. We felt weak and full of anxiety, and we could not pull our eyes off those banks of fog that now grazed us as they trotted in the opposite direction along the sides of the car, *something* despicable, an awful presence – quick, damp, breathless, terrible.

If someone were to have told us that Montelepre was located at a bend in the road, and was a town awash in pink with the green of kitchen gardens beneath a clear blue sky, and was a human town, stony too, yet full of human faces, we would have looked at him uncomprehendingly. Yet, after a few moments the most unthinkable thing of that morning occurred. As suddenly as it had appeared, the fog was gone, and to our right, beyond the curve of the road, shined the light pink tinged with the green and white of a large village. Further in the distance, beyond a small green area, you could see another town, tiny Giardinello, while on the left, further away, stone, and in the middle of the stone lay Partinico.

The car had stopped again. We could not believe our eyes. Looking to the left, a short, low wall, some cypress mixed with tall, almost black trees attracted our attention. On each side of a gate framed in a pedi-ment, which was supported by two columns and had two stone eagles above it sitting with wings outspread towards the valley, stood two white stones with large letters that read: 'Montelepre Cemetery.' Outside the low wall, where it turned, a tall, slender young man in shirtsleeves was intent on digging out some rocks with a spade. A ditch stretched out at his feet. Wiping his face with the underside of his arm, he looked at us. For a moment we were convinced he was about to speak. His lean, tanned face, with eyes that burned like two suns, quivered motionlessly. One could see the words run beneath his skin, like a fish underwater. Perhaps it was an age-old story, facing those rocks, the ditches. In the end, he lowered his eyes, but did not begin digging again right away. He was still watching us when the car started off again.

From above, before going down into the town, we began to see its steep streets, made of pebbles like knives, running narrow between the houses, of one storey or two at the most, no more solid than straw ricks or stables. You could also see some bell towers. Against the whiteness between one house and another, the black of a bull and the silver half-moon of its horns. Against the lime white of the houses, the black of open doors. Within the black of the doors, yellow faces.

Yellow and pale white faces were rushing all over then, in black, tri-angular shawls with a fringe border, over skirts and stockings and shoes that were entirely black too. In short, we no longer had any doubts – the town was full of black shawls, horses, light, silence. Beneath the shawls there were women in mourning, like all Mediter-ranean women. But here, in Montelepre, it was a particular kind of mourning, total and devoid of pity, hardened, like someone who suffers an offence more than a loss, obstinate like a subterranean feeling of revolt, pain beyond tears. It was not the home where the eldest son was lost, but the barracks of the irregular troops whose good captain fell in an ambush, delivering the town to the enemy with his death. Reason cried out that it was all absurd, that the town, like any town in the world, even the poorest and most isolated, could not be represented by a young man on bad terms with the law, and therefore that mourning and hardness were just custom and charac-ter. But something inside us, a secret antenna in lightning communi-cation with all the lairs and eyes of the village, told us over and over again that the emptiness and sense of loss and abandonment left by Giuliano were immense.

So we asked ourselves, as we had not done in so many years or in the few hours of fright that morning, who Giuliano was and what he might truly represent.

As we continued along the road and entered the town, the answer became unexpectedly clear and, though incredible, not in the least unfair and not in the least slanderous for anyone.

A large black animal, a wolf dog with a pointed muzzle and blood-shot eyes, powerful, free and calm, got up from the doorstep where he had been lying with his head resting on his paws, and leaned against the wall with a tolerance that conveyed being used to people, but did not bespeak friendship. His eyes were proud, full of darkness and fire whose shadows and sparks were upsetting. A little further off, another wolf was going down the stairs of the Town Hall. Two of them were lying in front of the Maria Santissima del Rosario Church. Others were going uphill, accompanying some children and goats along a narrow stony road. Although one wanted to justify their presence and omnipresence in the town with particular reasons, the mind continu-ally returned to a single thought, which was also supported by the old, often unsteady appearance of these animals with their guarded, dis-tressed looks. Besides wolves, you saw normal dogs, weakened by atrocious poverty, tremble imperceptibly, lying in the pale sunlight.

There were goats, donkeys, the sound of a trotting horse, the sight of a black horse, and cows, a bull passing by.

Behind all of the animals' steps and shapes and looks and breaths were the shawls, the white faces, the black eyes. There was nothing in those eyes while they stared at us. As soon as we passed by, if we happened to turn around to look, there were memory and hate that went beyond our persons, that went to the holy world of God, of which we were a part. Sometimes there was not even hate, not even a consciousness of our presence, but only boundless pain.

One woman was sitting inside a house, in front of a lamp and a picture. She had her hands in her lap, her eyes riveted like nails on the image. There, in that banal photograph framed in black, the figure of the young man standing straight in front of the Bellolampo barracks was repeated: the same blond hair, the wide face, the calm, hard eyes. The woman looked at it, as if talking. Other women were in one house or another, at one window or another, looking after one child or another, but with the same gloomy, shining eyes, the same face, withered by distant fires, and those worn-out hands. Everywhere, young or old, under the protection of the law or himself a representative of the law, the man of Montelepre was a stocky individual with a light-complexioned face, hard, distracted eyes; and the woman, a shadow – elusive, violent.

We went up to the Town Hall. The sordid, bare entry hall and the broken, dimly lit stairs were also full of women, with those immense shawls of theirs, flattened up against the wall. In the rooms on the first floor where the offices were, poorly furnished and dark, except for a few small lamps of little value, it appeared as if a war had just ended and, after the surrender of the city and living through the first terrible days, the women arrive to ask for work. We understood a lot of things, and one thing that we would never have suspected. First of all, about one hundred families had one of their own serving a life sentence or, in any case, feared they would, and in these families the mourning would never end again. Once more, the town was burned out, as in the wake of a violent occupation, and was fruitful only for some people. A few had put aside some money, and that too, for the most part, had ended up paying for court costs to help the 'picciotti,'[1] in absurd attempts to avert a hopeless sentence or to alleviate the sufferings of their dear ones. The hate between the two big families had seemingly dissolved in this sense of collective disaster that, like shame and hunger, had shot through the town clear to its roots. By then Pisciotta and Giuliano were no longer names of distinct, hostile fatality, but of misfortune, generated by the common desire for life. This desire for life, though distorted, immersed in crime, contrary to all the laws on the other side of the sea, was not felt by anyone as remorse. Rather, as regret.

No one in those rooms, in those offices, in other offices we entered, in the homes, the lanes, the stables, the churches, or in the few places where people were working, said the name Pisciotta or Giuliano in our presence. Above all, Giuliano. Giuliano – this is what all those hard, formidable looks said to us – was Montelepre, he was the people of Montelepre. He was the longing of a town imprisoned by the desert, by atrocious nature, the longing for freedom, happiness, life.

Like a wolf that is fatally wounded because, overcome by hunger, he slaughtered a lamb, Montelepre lay with its muzzle on the stone, looking high above. And its wan sky was still Giuliano.

NOTES

1 *Picciotto* is a dialect word that generally means young man. It is also used to indicate a young man associated with the Mafia.

Searching for Palermo

AMELIA CRISANTINO

For reasons Signora Olga could never entirely understand, her husband had always been grateful to a certain Don Vito Pispisa, who was born in their same home town and came to Palermo when the Americans arrived. This feeling traced back to a distant justification tied to circumstances that had brought both men to live and work in the city, and it now testified to the good heart and memory one of them possessed. 'So many other men in your place,' Signora Olga would always say to her husband, 'don't spend their entire lives showing their gratitude to someone.' On holidays, it was obligatory to take Don Vito a tray of homemade desserts prepared just for the occasion. A large bundle of *buccellati*[1] at Christmas, cannoli filled with the freshest ricotta for Carnival. Whenever they went back to their town, Signora Olga made some sweet, round pastries, filled with squash and honey, then topped with a dusting of powdered sugar, just for him. Nothing too involved, just those sweets that testified to an undying devotion, which Don Vito received with a simple nod of the head, as if it were perfectly natural. For his part, he never troubled to give gifts in return.

Signora Olga's husband had been called Don Pino for ages by then, at least by everyone whose dealings with him were bound by polite respect. However, there were some people who addressed him in that manner out of regard for his age, or to do the same thing other people did. Still others had reasons that went back a long time. Back then, as one could see in photographs taken of him around the time of their wedding, her husband had been a thin fellow with very dark skin, but the lack of sunlight and a sedentary job had transformed him into a corpulent man with a yellowish complexion. His face always had a dark shadow, even right after he shaved. An utterly ordinary man. A face you would mistake for a hundred others like it and instantly forget, which fit in perfectly among the heaps of requests and reminders that were gathering dust and had littered his desk for so long they had become permanent fixtures.

During the forty years he had put in at his job, he had had a perfectly normal career. When he was hired, they addressed him with the title of accountant. Now the two typists who worked in the office next to his called him doctor, but not because of allusions to any particular studies.

What remains to be explained is a certain familiarity which, inasmuch as the man's character – withdrawn, actually, and a little peevish – would allow, was expressed toward several individuals working in the Council Clerk's Office. Although they held positions with different levels of prestige and duties, they were united both by the fact they came from the same town, or at the very least its general locale, and by the devoted gratitude they all felt toward Don Vito Pispisa. They thought they owed him everything. Their job and career, but not only that. Their homes too, purchased with low rates, and business deals they had been able to make thanks to certain information. No specific results, it is true. Nothing that they could not have achieved on their own in other circumstances or places, but the story was very different there. For them, Don Vito promised little and did even less, but when he took on a task, people could reasonably hope to be satisfied. He was a man of few words. If they urged him to help, he would say, 'We'll see. We'll see what we can do now.' So, even when things just happened to turn out the way people wanted, he would reap all the credit, besides the glory, for himself.

But one must understand him too. To satisfy everyone he would have needed the Midas touch, because among so many people who dreamed of having a protector for just a moment, his clients had experienced what it meant to have one, and had awoken like sharks tasting blood. There was quite a bit of difference between what they would have liked to have and what they managed to obtain. What kept afloat their gratitude, which in lean times could run the risk of turning into resentment, was the consciousness that if they obtained little in those conditions, they would not have had anything in different ones.

So everyone was ready to rush to do something that would please Don Vito. They did not have relationships with each other and they did not think of themselves as his friends. They might have given it a bit of thought, because at that point it was rare for someone not to have his private Don Vito. If someone really was without one, then his cousin's or brother-in-law's was fine too, always trying, however, to keep it in the family, which is better for certain things.

If there was something detected by antennas made sensitive by personal interest and also a certain disinterested taste and disposition for trying to obstruct outsiders in any way, it was Don Pino they told. They would just happen to stop by his office, to hear what was in the air and talk over a few ideas with an older colleague who was an expert, something that did not break any regulations and did not compromise anyone. As they left, they asked him for a favour, mere trifles among people from the same town who put great store in not forgetting their friends. If by chance, but only if it so happened, for goodness sake, he absolutely should not go out of his way to do it, but if by chance he was going to meet Don Vito, then could he ask him to remember about that certain little matter that was making life difficult for his brother-in-law, the accountant? A trifle, such a small matter it was hardly worth bothering Don Vito, who, however, took care of annoying situations.

In Don Pino's office there was a daily coming and going of people who came to tell him about their departments' confidential business dealings and, once they were on familiar terms, gossip, malicious stories, and downright slanderous tales too, because that way the days go by more quickly and it is more enjoyable to meet with other people.

He listened to everything. Sitting back in his small armchair, made of green imitation leather, he tried to imitate Don Vito's air of studied calm. He hardly ever got up to welcome someone, but when he did, he moved with an agility you would not have suspected. He was quick to reach the door, and while he said, 'Come in, dear friend, come on in,' he would close his door, but not without popping his head out first to take a careful look up and down the hall. Not because it might be necessary. It was just a habit that he could not break. Then he would listen to all the things his visitors had to tell him. But what he enjoyed even more was watching them, because of their obvious desire to please him, which, he knew perfectly well, regarded his own person only in passing.

At home Don Pino had a large journal with a sturdy, rust-coloured cover. He had started keeping the journal years and years ago on Don Vito's advice because, as he used to say, 'You just never know. It's better to keep your back covered.' He diligently wrote notes, organized in alphabetical order, about facts and people who had attracted his attention during his day at the office. With years of time and practice he had become very skilful, demonstrating an ability that would have been entirely unexpected by anyone who was familiar with how slow and ostentatiously indifferent he was at his work. A maximum of three lines was devoted to whatever minor piece of news or important business matter he happened to record, and he had an unfailing intuition for grasping which facts, out of all the raw, shapeless material he had to choose from, would be of most interest to his patron.

Now and then when he went to visit Don Vito Pispisa, he brought along the journal, its pages covered with small writing and teeming with numbers, arrows, and reference marks. He would arrive and, when it was a good day, sit down in front of him at a small round table made of dark wood. The top of the table had a mosaic made entirely out of wood, with ever so many small pieces of inlay, some of which must have been almost white at one time, and the others dark, forming definite designs. Time and grease had now turned them all the same colour, leaving one only to guess at what was beneath the dark patina. After being shown into the room to wait for Don Vito, Don Pino would become completely absorbed in trying to make out the old contours and then give up angrily because he could never be sure about the original pattern. It had become an obsession.

Some days, as he walked down the street that led from his house to Don Vito's, he repeated to himself that this time at least he was not going to look for the design, but he could hardly ever resist. As soon as he arrived, he strained his eyes and mind in that secret act of dogged determination. He could tell that there were shapes and then he would become lost searching for the details. If he isolated one corner, he sometimes felt he was on the verge of grasping the meaning of it all together, but there was always some detail on the opposite side that distracted his attention. When he made up his mind to insert it in the design, it did not fit. As he went back to take a close look at the shapes he had first intuited, the contours that he had worked so hard to isolate broke furiously apart before his eyes, rolling away in so many disconnected signs with no sense at all, and it was no longer possible to put them together again. Finally, when Don Vito arrived, he would put his briefcase on top of the table to prevent himself from seeing it anymore.

Seated at that table, they spoke in gestures and tones of voice that out of a habit formed over so many years made them seem like old friends. But each of them well knew his own place, starting with the fact that though both of them suffered more or less from the aches and pains of rheumatism, by tacit agreement the chair standing in the corner between two walls was reserved for Don Vito, and the chair facing it was Don Pino's. Headed toward this spot was a light stream of air originating from several badly sealed cracks, which, due to the play of the currents, would gather up all the small stirrings of air in the room and then dissipate like a will-o'-the wisp right there on that chair, not daring to advance toward the corner. On windy days, which were many, it could become a truly piercing draft that struck at the nape of the unfortunate victim occupying that seat, yet Don Pino never had the nerve to complain about it.

Don Vito inquired about everything. He listened to news from the Council Clerk's Office, but never forgot about their town or even to ask Don Pino about things at home and his neighbours too. Apart from the work that he had to do – and he had proved himself to be a master at tying together threads, acquaintances, and pieces of information that, at first glance, seemed so far removed – he also had a disinterested love of knowledge, a will to know everything about everyone else just for the sake of knowing, without any ulterior motives. Sometimes it just so happened later that from this reserve of the most disparate, scattered bits of news, memories of things were pulled out that were useful for jamming up one person or intimidating someone else. Which goes to show that knowledge and learning, if well directed, are hardly ever useless in the end. Don Pino had always thought it was opportune, right, and also more prudent to follow scrupulously the advice that Don Vito gave on the most disparate subjects, always with the clear certainty that he would later be satisfied. While Don Pino listened to him, it seemed as if Don Vito saw through the apparent motives for things, and, even though he had never set foot in the Council Clerk's Office, knew its innermost workings, so much so that he connected men, dates, and facts in a way that never failed to amaze Don Pino. He of all people certainly did not need the journal, he had an entire archive in his head.

Of all the things Don Pino envied about Don Vito, what he envied even more than the strong, artfully woven web of favours and blackmail was the calm, assured way of acting he had achieved, which he played and exhibited with conscious ease. While watching him, Don Pino would forget the patience necessary for getting results, his eyes acquired an innocence never fully possessed, and he fell into the role the other man assigned to him.

There were moments when he was alone in the room with Don Vito, the sole spectator for such a show, and it seemed as if everything were born from and moved by that man's desire, that somehow the strength of things that were known drove other things to become what he wanted them to be. It was an awesome spectacle, and how! For a long moment it seemed as if the things that went on happening outside were not so important anymore. Everything would be worked out somehow.

Don Pino observed that ostentatious calm, that sign of the achievement of power, with much deeper admiration because he knew things had not always been like that. If he thought about it, he could still see Don Vito as a young man who used to run across the fields and then hurry down to the city, where he controlled all the goods coming from his area to the black market. Quick, determined, a far cry from the remote serenity he now loved to display. He did not trust anyone else, always running to take care of things himself, knocking himself out with work. Thanks to the Americans he had become rich, well known, valued, in a word, powerful. They made him. Without the occupation he would have been no one.

My, what a great opportunity that was, something unique for the young men biting at the bit who wanted to get rich quick, right away, because they were living a magical moment, and no one could tell how things would go when it was over. They continued to go well, but not like before. It took more patience, more work; things did not move along so quickly anymore. Don Vito showed he was on the ball. He started from almost nothing and made himself in just a few years. Always on the spot wherever he might be needed, he had the will to bide his time before making choices, and the luck to hit on the best decisions.

He had met so many people, made the right friends, had a good memory, and this helped him. He never forgot those who did him a wrong, but not the ones who gave him a hand either, and he was a master at having news that could do him good get around. This way he was forming a small group of his own, which was not even different from the many other small groups that were everywhere at that time.

His stature started to grow in other peoples' estimation, and in his own, when even those who were not involved with him referred to the people around him as 'Don Vito's men.' He knew for sure that he had made a name for himself when the hope for the advantages that knowing him brought drove the relatives and friends of people he had helped to come to him, to ask for favours and help, and to put themselves at his disposal. That was when he put on the air of godfather because, even though he knew there was still so much work to do, and that just annoying someone was all it would take to never succeed, all those people who turned to him and seemed to expect that with a nod or a word everything would be taken care of, all this was proof he was becoming important. They believed in him. And even if he had no idea how to do something, even if he knew perfectly well he could not fix a certain matter, he was always scrupulous about putting himself at others' disposal all the same, and then he really did his utmost, or he helped them in other circumstances that he could manage more easily. Then, he was also very careful to see that the manoeuvres that came out well became known, because this was what his name's good fortune depended upon.

It did not take much for him to begin really feeling powerful, and little by little he modelled his face on God Almighty. Those who knew him and had seen him running all over the countryside, sweating and killing himself over obtaining one man's silence and the protection of another, still could not take that face seriously. That only happened when word got around that for certain things that had happened, animals killed and worse, he was the one you had to see. He understood at once that nothing is more useful than these things for teaching respect and keeping everyone in his own place.

Don Pino had been there for Don Vito's ascent from the very beginning, sportingly admired and not competitive at all, aware as he was that he was not made of the same stuff anyway. His kind of devotion was beyond reproach, and he felt privileged if he could be of use to Don Vito.

Many years later, when things had turned out really well and in the eyes of those who had just arrived on the scene it seemed as if Don Vito's power had existed forever and solidly extended into the future, Don Pino knew that he was the only one who knew the true story. Every time he thought about it he could only feel won over by Don Vito's climb up the ladder. 'If there were a manual for this kind of thing, it would be a perfect case,' he would say to himself, sincerely annoyed that so much talent, steadfastness, and fortune could not be publicly singled out as an example for younger people. Don Pino elab-

orated a brief recapitulation that took into account the most important points.
1) Don Vito started from nothing and without any help, even though a lot of help arrived later.
2) He had staked his life on a place where no one was willing to give up on their own accord even a crumb of what they had.
3) He had stayed in the shadows. Beyond his own circle and the circle of his friends, no one had ever heard of him.
4) He had taken a big risk from the start, because it is always a risk to put aside one's habits and tested means of protection and to say 'I,' most of all where everyone looks for the slightest opening to appear, in order to scramble on and climb up.
5) It went well for him.
Don Pino smiled, pleased with himself. He thought that such a lucid ability for synthesis was not easy to achieve.

Sitting in an armchair, her feet resting on a small table set in front of her, with a cucumber hydra-toner mask on her face, Ida Benelli was flipping through a magazine in the kitchen of her home. Her hair was wrapped in a white towel, her face covered with a thick layer of light green gel that gave her a sensation of well-being.
'The latest summer fashions. Pouf skirts for women over 100 pounds? Two fashion experts give their answers. Desserts to prepare in 40 minutes. What your skin needs over forty. The biggest danger to your fresh complexion – free radicals, difficult to stop and neutralize. Day and night skin treatments with the most advanced scientific research.' She already knew everything they could have written, but read the article clear to the end. She was starting to find that magazine depressing, every two pages there was some ad for an anti-wrinkle cream. She continued to flip through the pages without even pausing until she came to an article in the series 'Great Italian Cities,' titled 'Living in Palermo.' Photographs of the Politeama, Mondello, and then shops, neighbourhood festivals, and wooden puppets. Where to shop, the best places to eat, insider addresses for restaurants serving the best fish, the latest artisan studios.
The magazine had articles on current news, fashion, and culture for the up-to-date, dynamic woman, so it also alluded to the less desirable aspect of the city. But without being too heavy-handed; women readers want to be informed, but not to the point of boredom. Even amidst difficulties, urban renewal continues. Projects in the historic

downtown area are starting up; they are ridding the city of the rubble left by the war.

The mayor standing among children in a school on the outskirts of the city. Be as it may, it is a rich city and money is circulating, the city with the highest sales of high-horsepower cars. The stores are more luxurious than Milan's. All's well that ends well.

She stopped reading, set the magazine on her legs, and lit a cigarette, lost in thought. She remembered something she had read who knows where, that Palermo is the city where it can happen that, from one day to the next, a butcher turns up buying an entire building for hundreds and hundreds of thousands of lire. There were even examples, all of them about people who met a bad end.

And those who succeeded instead? One rarely heard about them; if the case did not explode wide open, the silence of people around them was guaranteed. Money. That was the wall she ran into for all her plans. It was close, too close. At times she had had a lot of plans, but never knew what the future had in store for her. An exasperating uncertainty that was surely not good for either her health or mood.

To move to another home, to move to another neighbourhood. Penthouses, to lord over the noise below, to have the city at her feet.

She had been in one of these dream homes one afternoon, to play cards. An acquaintance of hers had taken her. She was ready to bestow full honours upon the lady of the house, for having attained so much. Instead, she found a nitwit before her eyes. Parquet floor, rugs, cork panelling on the walls, a lot of ceramic pottery scattered here and there, the terrace full of plants, of scents, the maid a woman of colour who fit perfectly in the stage design. A dream. The entire time she was there she closely studied the gestures and words of the women around her, trying to guess the secret of that success. It seemed a mystery. They did not come from rich families, one can tell these things right away, before a woman even opens her mouth. As for initiative, they did not even have enough to discard the right card. With all this, they were rich and she was not. There is no justice. It is really true.

She looked at the clock to check how much time was left for the mask, still a couple of minutes. She settled back in the chair and closed her eyes.

To become rich. Some of the people she knew had succeeded, and there were so many others she had heard about.

'Certainly one can always steal, but it's horribly risky. You need accomplices, the right information. You need to be professionals. If not, they nab you right away.

'Become a money lender. Takes too long. You need capital to start up, and someone who could guarantee that the money is paid back later. Too complicated, you need someone who knows how to make people respect him. You expose yourself personally.

'Blackmail. It's the best system, the tidiest, the quickest. I'd be great!'

Her eyes still closed, Ida Benelli stretched in the chair and smiled at herself while she thought, 'It would really be exciting. Not exposing yourself, not revealing who you are. It's happened so many times that a blackmailer has been killed.' She instantly remembered the scenes from countless American movies. Blackmailers killed with guns, poisons, knives, tampered brakes and down over the mountainside. No pity for them, there's always someone who says, 'Die, dirty black-mailer.' Badly shaven guys or women with caked-on make-up. You dislike them immediately.

'A beautiful blackmail scheme. Like everything, it's just a question of being organized. What it takes to succeed:

a) Do everything possible so the person being blackmailed doesn't know who you are, otherwise your fate is sealed.

b) A disguised voice on the phone. A place that's impossible to control for the money drop. The train station? In the end, you have to come out in the open at all costs.

c) Establish contact without making any mistakes.

d) Act alone, never trust an accomplice. They're the lowest sort.'

She was not persuaded. Too many conditions, and all of them important ones. Not to mention that you need to have an exclusive on a good secret, something profitable, that can ruin someone who has a lot of money. Or someone, in any case, who would be able to get it. Naturally, it does not happen every day that you find out about something like that.

There's certainly heroin, a sure thing for making money. Selling drugs, getting your hands dirty, something everybody would know about right away. Compromising yourself. And for how much money? They never become more than retailers. Be a courier. No, too danger-ous. You have to expose yourself personally. Stuff for the real down-and-outs. All those housewives who ended up in the newspapers.[2] You couldn't say they got rich.

She thought of the story that Signora Giuseppina had told her in tears, about a niece of hers caught carrying drugs. She swore up and down, saying the girl didn't know anything about it, she was going to visit some relatives. She was carrying that suitcase just to do a favour for a friend who, in turn, was paying off a debt with one of his brother-in-law's cousins. It was unbelievable. They had to have made a mistake, changed suitcases, certainly she knew absolutely nothing whatever, who could be so evil they would hate them so much. Ida Benelli smiled at the thought of that scene, so much naivety was even touching. Nothing to do about it, too many risks. The shame of that sort of story could fall on the whole family. Signora Giuseppina did nothing but explain herself and justify things. After she had told everyone about her misfortunes she went into a period of mourning and did not show her face around anymore. It was better that way, with her constantly racking herself to the point of tears, always saying 'What a disgrace ...' with her gloomy face. It made the situation embarrassing for everyone.

The ideal thing would be to invest money in drug trafficking, staying far removed and clean, untouchable. Fabulous profits. She did not remember anymore how much a million lire[3] would make, but it was an incredible sum. Something that with a couple of million lire you become millionaires. The best deal imaginable, absolutely.

The only problem is how to do it, who to give the money to, to invest. What a really good idea it would be, but how does one go about it? If the profits are so high there's no need for anyone else to get into the racket. This is the only real problem.

She got up and went to wash off her face.

Ida Benelli gave a start as she read the headline that the *L'Ora* newspaper ran on the first page. She knew that name. She went up to the newsstand and looked at the photograph. She recognized Mariannina standing among her crying relatives next to the male murder victim. She bought the newspaper.

She leaned against the wall, stopping to read, something a respectable woman should never do. So, they had killed the brother of her old friend, her schoolmate and ex-neighbour. She read the article clear to the end. Ties with shady characters, speculations about the motive. Mafia families, territorial rivalries. She did not really keep up with topics of that sort, and could not follow the names that intersected or the list of distant places that everyone nevertheless seemed to frequent. When someone went to Canada, relatives and friends who came before him or after were sure to pop up immediately. So it even happened that some people died far away from their own land.

Ida Benelli had a very quick mind and was practical by nature, two things that had always come in useful. She started to walk again, reflecting upon what she had read and immediately putting it to profitable use.

'Mariannina's brother is dead. Who would ever have thought that he was mixed up in these things,' she thought. 'Who knows if they were able to make some money. That's clearly why someone gets mixed up in such matters. Then they wind up killing him. Maybe they killed him just because he was the friend of some other guy. A really senseless death. In any case, his friends would take care of avenging him. At least one hopes so. And what about the widow? In the movies they always help her. Perhaps I ought to renew my ties with Mariannina again.

'It certainly was a blow, but with one brother dead, there are still five other brothers and two sisters. I'm sorry for them, but the moment is right. If they hadn't killed him, I never would have known that being on familiar terms with her could be useful. It's better that way. And then, one knows from the start that trafficking drugs is risky. It's useless to pretend otherwise and give in to despair. It's always a pity, but it's a big family.

'I'm going to pay a visit on my old friend, offer my solidarity, and see if there's a way for me to get into trafficking. A couple of jobs and I'll retire immediately, before things heat up too much. Dangerous. But if it goes well, as long as I'm alive I'm sitting pretty.'

NOTES

1 *Buccellati* are a fried pastry, generally rolled in honey, sugar, and toasted almonds.
2 The reference to the housewives ending up in the newspapers likely alludes to the pronounced trend in the 1980s, when women, generally of the lower class, with large families, were used as 'mules' to transport drugs from Palermo to New York.
3 One million lire would be approximately five hundred dollars.

The *Truvatura*[1]

SILVANA LA SPINA

It took four people to hold back his mother. She was blinded by pain, and deaf to everything but the silence of the quarry on the edge of the Margherito district. Even the cicadas were hushed. Even the snakes ceased their rustling for a long stretch of land. Everything was still, like a gloomy sacristy painting.

The little boy was laying on his side, with one leg bent under his tiny body. It looked as if he were sleeping, but that position was far too unnatural to reconcile with the sleep of children. Except for eternal sleep.

'Marshal, look!' the brigadiere pointed his yellowish finger, stained by *Nazionale* cigarettes, towards a fissure at the base of the cave wall. The dirt was freshly turned and dark, as if someone had recently been digging in that area.

'What could it mean?' he said softly. As both Marshal Di Blasi and Brigadiere Miccichè walked over to investigate the spot, they were blinded by the unrelenting, merciless sun, deafened by the mother's screams, and bothered by the throng of curious onlookers crowding around. It seemed as if the entire town had set out towards the countryside, a bit out of solidarity, but mostly out of unhealthy curiosity.

'Someone has been digging over here,' the marshal confirmed.

The brigadiere, who had arrived at that conclusion from the very first moment, simply said yes, sir. But he could not resist the desire to point out the hoe and shovel left further back, against the cave wall.

'It's clear the killer wanted to bury the boy. He even made a cross.'

In fact, the sign of the cross was crudely drawn in chalk on the cave wall, right above the shovelled dirt. The brigadiere traced the white cross with his yellowish finger, and at the bottom of it came upon a spider's web. His finger broke it mercilessly.

'I'm not convinced,' he said under his breath, but not so softly that the marshal could not hear him.

'Instead, it's clear as can be to me.'

'Someone who kills like that, marshal, doesn't worry about giving a Christian burial. And also, the cross is too precise of a sign. It almost says "look here below."'

In the darkness of the cave their eyes met, the marshal's expression slightly mocking and the brigadiere's dark and impassive, as if he had lentils in place of eyes.

'Maybe at the last minute the killer's Christian convictions won out,' insisted the marshal stubbornly.

'In this town of barbarians!' The brigadiere was even more stubborn.

'If I'm not mistaken, you must be from these parts too.'

'Exactly.'

Nearly the entire town went to the funeral. The small white coffin emerged from the church, carried by a few relatives and the boy's older brothers. Then came his father and mother, not a tear left in their eyes, his sister Annuzza, followed by his fourth-grade schoolmates, dressed in their school smocks, freshly ironed for the occasion.

It was hell for the little children. It was almost summer and their black smocks sucked up the heat as if it were ink. But their teacher watched over them threateningly – woe to anyone who leaves the procession and goes off to the countryside to climb trees and gather green almonds.

The brigadiere's son was allowed to carry the flag, but at the church door the privilege was about to slip into other small hands. It ended up in a brawl, and the teacher had to intervene. She was crying, calling them selfish little wretches. That crying was more violent than a slap, since her tears were unjustified. Vincenzo certainly was not a nice schoolmate. He used to steal the mortadella out of their sandwiches, and his homework had more ink smears than words. More than once the teacher had sent him to stand behind the chalk board, and each time she put the paper hat with donkey's ears on his head.

'What was Vincenzo like?' the brigadiere had asked his son that same morning.

The boy kept playing with his cup of milk, which he detested, hoping with all his heart that it would curdle and finally the cat would drink it.

'He'd say dirty words a lot.'

'More than the others?'

'No,' the boy answered honestly, 'like everyone else.'

'You too?'

The little boy looked him in the face with that expression that always worried Brigadiere Miccichè because of the way it resembled how he was thirty years ago. In fact, every time his son looked at him like that, it seemed as if he were standing in front of a mirror.

'Sometimes when I get bad grades,' and he held out his notebook of summaries.

The brigadiere thumbed through the notebook, sighing, until he reached the last pages, marked sadistically by a big 'D' in blue pencil.

'It seemed like it was good to me,' the little boy justified himself, again starting to stir his milk with the spoon.

Miccichè read those four little pages, somewhat aghast at his first-born's enviable ability to make use of a language all his own, not to be found in any dictionary (Miccichè was one of those rare carabinieri who use the dictionary), and which could be considered Italian only by a long stretch of imagination. But precisely for this reason, it had a certain charm, and was adorned with all the onomatopoeic words that the boy had managed to find in the life of the town, where two thousand people and as many donkeys and sheep lived. After some effort, he finally understood that the assignment was some kind of summary of a passage from the novel *Tom Sawyer*. It was the part in which Tom and Becky get lost in the caves during a field trip. His son must have been so fascinated by the remote possibility that he might happen to have the same adventure (after all, in the story Tom was also far from being a saint) that he made a crude map of the labyrinth where the characters get lost, to go along with his incomprehensible summary. He was struck by the cross drawn at one spot.

'Why did you put this cross here?' he asked, astonished. He had never read *Tom Sawyer*. His family had never had money to spend on children's books – a pair of shoes every other year to celebrate the Day of the Dead was already a lot.

'This is the place where Indian Joe hid the treasure,' his son preened, and seeing that his father was lost in thought, he cautiously began to pour the rest of his milk into the cat's bowl.

'So why didn't you mention it in your assignment?'

The little boy looked confused. 'I did. Only I called it the *truvatura*. It seemed to fit better. We aren't Americans,' he concluded with a sigh aimed at the teacher's absurd pretensions.

Walking outside in the sun, the brigadiere now saw that word flash before his eyes, along with the pebbles that people in the procession kicked on the way to the cemetery. Like everyone else, he knew what a *truvatura* was, just as he knew that the *fimmini i notti* were a kind of witch who braid the hair of sleeping newborn babies so they won't reach a year of age. For fear of these Eringes of folklore, no one dared to cut the bewitched hair of their babies before they were a year old. Even his wife, who as a kindergarten teacher considered herself evolved, had not gone against the superstition, using the sparse down that the baby had in place of hair as justification. But of all the legends of sorcery and witchcraft, the *truvatura* was the one that no one uttered out of tacit convention, held back because it involved the sacrifice of a victim whose blood would favour the discovery, or *truvatura*, of a great treasure.

But there it was again. The memory of that cross on the cave wall a few steps from little Vincenzo returned, and reappeared before him. Yet again, this image was superimposed with the crude map drawn in his son's good school notebook, which, despite the topographic skill, did not save it from the teacher's 'D.'

'I found out something this morning,' the marshal suddenly said at his side.

'What?'

At that moment, the town band blared out, playing as loud and off-key as it possibly could. No one ever knew what tune those ten musicians, dressed up in black wool suits recalling Fascist uniforms, might be playing, but that was also because the generous, deafening sound of the cymbals ended up drowning everything out.

'The Percolla family had sent the marriage broker Donna Agatina to ask for the hand of Annuzza, the dead boy's sister.'

'Annuzza's beautiful,' murmured the brigadiere. He could never pull his eyes away from her Titian hair, to their pure delight.

'And the Percollas are mafiosi,' replied the marshal. 'They'd wash the refusal away with blood.'

'They'd only need to have the girl kidnapped,' pointed out the brigadiere. 'Without having to kill her brother. And then who's to say Annuzza would turn down the marriage.' He motioned towards the young Percolla, who stepped to the front of the procession to give the young woman support in her time of grief.

'I have eyes too,' snapped the marshal. 'But it had to be someone.'

'I might have an idea.'

'Just what we needed,' sighed the marshal, taking off his hat and wiping away the sweat with his handkerchief.

By then they had arrived at the cemetery.

'To what do I owe the honour, brigadiere?'

Before he answered, Miccichè waited for the parish priest to take off his white, lace-bordered vestment in his usual rough manner.

'I was looking for the sacristan.'

The priest peered at him over the garment. 'And why?'

The brigadiere skirted the question in an entirely natural way that was, as always, entirely artificial, and worked to perfection, especially with the parish priest. The church, as everyone knows, adores artifice. The result was a question, shot point-blank, about superstitions that the church was still not able to eradicate completely.

'For example?' asked the priest attentively.

'The *truvatura*,' the brigadiere said nonchalantly.

The priest looked perplexed, and then burst out laughing. 'Nobody believes in that anymore, except Sarino. These days people prefer to bet on soccer games if they really hope to get rich quick.'

'Or else they take up racketeering or hide stolen goods for criminals.'

'Who are you referring to?' the priest asked sharply.

'No one. There've been some rumours.'

Just rumours, but unpleasant, disturbing ones. Some of them were about the parish priest, and how he aided and abetted people from the city, hiding their loot, if not other things, on the land he owned in the Margherito district. More than once the brigadiere had rushed over to that area to check out the rumours, and every time he came up empty-handed. He felt a sense of disgrace, because even though he was a faithful Catholic, like everyone in the armed forces, Miccichè could not stand the new parish priest. He was always immersed in matters concerning material things, always quarrelling with his relatives over the inheritance of an uncle who was an estate leaseholder.[2] The whole thing irritated Miccichè even more because he compared him to the old parish priest, good as gold, always ready to help his fellow townspeople if they were in trouble. But this was a different matter, of course, to consider in due time and with proof in hand. So before the other thread slipped through his fingers, he returned to the *truvatura*.

His thoughts raced to that half-wit Sarino, the sacristan. For years he had bragged about knowing the place where there was an enormous treasure, which he would lay his hands on in due time. But since no one knew when it would happen, as time went by, the story became a joke. In fact, 'uncle Sarinu's *truvatura*' had become a popular saying in town for promising the moon. Even the brigadiere used it when his son asked for something too steep for his pockets. To his 'When will you buy it for me, papa?' he'd reply, laughing, 'The day I discover uncle Sarinu's *truvatura*.' Now that joke could not even bring a smile to his face. In fact, it made a strange shiver run up his spine, which had nothing to do with the dank darkness of the sacristy.

'What can you tell me about Sarino?' he finally asked, almost with effort.

'What's there to say?' the priest sighed with relief. 'If you can imagine, he becomes even more of an idiot by the day. The children don't give him a moment's peace. I want to tell you the latest thing that happened.'

The priest actually told him something about the sacristan's peculiar mentality that was not of this world or the next. Although he was not a true idiot, he was nevertheless short-witted, and thus the object of the children's cruel jokes.

'Was little Vincenzo with those children too?'

The priest's eyes became heavy. It seemed as if his long gaze bore the weight of a millstone as he looked slowly around the sacristy.

'Yes. He was there,' he whispered.

The parish priest spent almost all the afternoon in the darkness of the sacristy, as if drowning in the depths of an anguish that he could not escape. He did not stir until it was time for the Angelus. Then he stood up, put the vestment back on, and walked wearily towards the altar. It seemed as if he had aged ten years. Fortunately, the handful of little old ladies, almost blind as bats, did not notice a thing.

Strangely enough, that afternoon Sarino did not make even one false move during the ritual, and when he closed the church door, he was extremely courteous.

'Sarino!' called the priest.

The sacristan was carrying the candle-snuffer. In the naked light of the bulb hanging from a cord, it cast a long shadow on the ground. 'What's wrong?' he asked, thoughtlessly brandishing the snuffer as if it were a weapon.

'Sit down!'

'I'm sitting now.'

The parish priest pretended to straighten up his desk, but was actually biding time. He did not know where to begin.

'I'm giving you some advice. Disappear!' he finally said softly.

Sarino shuddered. 'Why?'

'The brigadiere thinks it was you who killed Vincenzo.'

'I thought about it sometimes. He always used to make the sign of the idiot at me when I passed by,' and he made the insulting hand gesture for idiot. 'But thinking isn't killing.'

The priest nodded his head. 'It's not because he called you an idiot. It's because you wanted the *truvatura*.'

'Oh, the *truvatura*,' said Sarino, astonished. 'Sure, sure. Someone like Vincenzo could have been very useful. Who knows if someone thought of it.'

'You thought of it.'

Sarino's disappearance served to confirm the brigadiere's grim suspicions. The next day a lot of the children did not go to school, and the ones who did were then kept inside at home all afternoon. The task was hardly devoid of difficulties and whining. Nothing fascinates children more than a child killer, especially if its fabled image was linked with the sacristan's half-witted face, which everyone had made fun of for generations. No one noticed that through this transformation, Sarino's image had taken on something diabolical, becoming a sort of evil giant who had dressed himself up in fool's clothing the better to deceive them all.

Using different words and much less imagination, a journalist who came from the city explained the matter. But as always, he preferred to force the issue of the taint of age-old superstitions. To better illustrate all this, he filled two entire rolls of film with the faces of a few old people, caught unawares on their doorsteps. He was convinced that all future pandemonium could be read even on their faces.

As for little Vincenzo's family (as every reader who takes the trouble to look through the same newspaper's archives can see), they were celebrities in those days. In a front-page article published in a well-known newspaper, a scholar researching folk traditions expounded upon the incident in light of old-fashioned Greek hubris, rather than as a normal case of crime. Annuzza appeared in the photographs for just what she was – a madonna of the people with the body of a pagan goddess. Some fourth-rate cineaste even contacted her. The young woman conveyed a reply urging him to respect her time of grief. And after all, she was engaged.

'Let's hope you find him soon,' remarked Miccichè's wife, stung that no one had mentioned her husband's name during the entire affair.

'We'll find him,' was all the brigadiere said.

They really did find him. One week later. He was already rotting, hanging from an olive tree on a rope that had taken off half his neck, his black tongue pecked by birds.

Vincenzo's family, for a moment seeing themselves deprived of the vendetta that was rightfully theirs, pronounced judgment: 'Let's leave him there, for the sun and worms to eat!' But then the father himself said to cut him down. Afterwards, he shut himself away in mourning again.

However, it was not clear where to bury him. The sacristan had no one, and furthermore he had committed two crimes, one against his fellow man and one against himself, as the parish priest explained. No one even mentioned burying him in the church cemetery.

'Let's bury him right here,' someone said, and it seemed the sensible thing to do. Only then did they realize that Sarino had hung himself not far from where his victim had been found, and thus not far from the cave where he had imagined the riches that he had always dreamed of – the *truvatura* – would be. This coincidence sealed his doom, and denied no one the chance for a personal remark, even the most trite and the most malevolent.

'The murderer always returns to the scene of the crime,' was the gloss provided by the town clerk at the club. Everyone nodded admiringly in agreement because as a boy the clerk had studied at the seminary, and necessarily had to know more about things than the rest of them.

They met in the dark and said nothing for a while, immersed in the viscous flow of their thoughts. Just every so often they restlessly shifted position in their chairs, and the creaking echoed sinisterly.

'I bet after all that's happened, no one will dare set foot in the Margherito district again,' an elderly man's soft voice finally said.

'Let's hope so. Certainly the boy's death should put a stop to the nasty habit of sticking their noses into other people's business,' the other man replied. 'Who'd you find out from that the boy had seen the trucks arrive?'

'From him. He told my son, and my son told me. We were just in time. Take, for example, if he'd said something about it at school. The brigadiere's son would have talked about it at home, and then amen,' he added, snickering 'as someone would say.'

'But the family, are you sure ...'

'I'm sure. I'm sure. Also, they have other things to think about. In fifteen days my son is marrying Annuzza. We Percollas do things in a big way. Don't forget! I want a beautiful wedding.'

'Have I ever disappointed you, by any chance?'

'Never, parish father,' snickered the elderly mafioso. 'I'm sorry about the sacristan. He got mixed up in this through no fault of his own. But we certainly couldn't let him live.'

The parish priest let out a sigh that got lost in the dark sacristy, bumping against the plaster saints and the madonnas that were wrapped up in paper shrouds, awaiting the processions.

'Sarino was just an idiot.'

NOTES

1 *Truvatura*, in Sicilian dialect, is the discovery of enchanted treasure.
2 In the Italian text, the word *gabelloto* is used, which indicates a person who holds the leases on large estate properties belonging, in general, to absentee landlords. In writings of and about Sicily, the word carries another nuance, because the leaseholders were infamous for Mafia associations.

The Mafia at My Back

LIVIA DE STEFANI

Mafia in the air and mafiosi in flesh and blood

I think I have already mentioned the strange uneasiness that I felt emanating from the Virzì estate even before I began to take care of running the property, which was located in a far west as mysterious and laden with perils as the hereafter of the Pillars of Hercules.[1] A sensation of 'geographic' danger, fully confirmed by my experience in the place. It was the same experience for everyone, for me as the owner and for the entire bunch of my workers, of being under a sort of hidden dictator. Everyone was governed by his unspoken orders.

Reaching me straight from the mouths of the estate administrator, the field guard, and the land leaseholders were names of arrogant middlemen, shifty commodity buyers, and undesired witnesses to some mischief committed by this or that peasant, whom I liked so very much. Symptoms that I took care of hastily and gave little if any thought to. Just as out of innate boldness I did not observe any of the rules of caution governing this field in Mafia territory. I lived life rashly, whether in Rome or down there, always. Giving absolutely no heed to danger, I forged on with my head held high right up till the end. For no other serious reason, I believe, than to win a bet with myself. Really. Back then in the country and towns, women were considered just slightly above hens by the men. I think I was the first woman who was able to oppose the rural Mafia's plans, running no danger they would hurt a hair on my head. Not because of the fact I was a person of the female sex, and therefore undeserving of consideration. Quite the contrary, because for those individuals, as the owner of Virzì I was a pawn of primary importance for them on their chessboard of power games, which were directly aimed at the conquest of my land. I could see the fire burning in their eyes, like ravenous wolves, fixed on Virzì and just waiting to attack at the first sign of me giving in, and to devour it in one gulp, paying next to nothing.

I had understood, and so it became necessary to be on the alert, to suspect everything and everyone. A horrible prospect. I ask myself, half a century later, what the first concrete fact was that led me to suppose I was entangled in the snares of the Mafia. From so far away, the glimmer of a symptom reaches me. Or, to be more precise, the glimmer of something strange.

The strange thing happened on the first night, when darkness first set on me at the Virzì country house, and I reproached the old field guard, Vincenzo L., because night had already fallen and he had neglected to double-lock the main door of the large courtyard. Between human beings and animals, a hundred defenceless creatures were living there. With his head lowered, he softly answered, whether out of prudence or resignation I would not know, *'Ccà nun c'è bisogno d'inserrare 'u purtuni,'*[2] a fundamentally mysterious proposition that allows me to testify to the survival of the Mafia in the thirties, the time when the phenomena of sinister Mafia interference inside the large landed estates had seemingly disappeared. The multi-centuries-old Mafia of the baronies, the town councils, and smuggling, which had always been as extremely powerful as the Mafia tentacles around the cities today, was really still operating – very slowly, but using its old tactics, in the triangle of the Palermo, Trapani, and Agrigento provinces, the most desirable ones.

Down there, the estate administrator was responsible primarily for the bookkeeping and paying the taxes, and the dealings with the buyers of agricultural goods. Then there was the field guard. He had the 'right to carry a shotgun,' which is to say, the right to carry a double-barrel shotgun, good for shooting dead anyone up to no good, pilferers, and nosy intruders. In reality, he was the first in command over my workers, and my property. Last in line after the administrator and field guard was the overseer, that is, the person in charge of watching over the population in the large courtyard, including the draught and farmyard animals. These were important people in my employ who were essentially paid a salary and owed me, if not complete obedience, at least gratitude for the faith I placed in them. Yet I sensed that they had to answer for their own behaviour also, or primarily, to others. In short, that they were other bosses' intermediaries, living on my estate.

It must be kept in mind that I was a woman, and therefore, in their mind's eye, a creature that was below the goat and chicken, incapable of managing anything. My dealings with both the field guard and the overseer were always filtered through the administrator. I felt like a deaf-mute. The leaseholders did not come to discuss the dates for the grain or grape harvests directly with me, nor did the peasants come to pay me directly what they owed for the land they worked. They did not converse with me. Why should they have if I was a woman? Just a woman. I did not have a father anymore, because my wonderful papa had died of a heart attack in 1936. My brother Peppino never showed his face around my parts; he was not the type to interfere in other people's business, even one of his sisters. After my husband's initial curiosity in the anthropological surprises that distant borderland of Italy held, he did not venture to Virzì anymore. I was a woman all alone, stuck in the middle of men's problems, without the help of any encouragement, even a smile. Alone, in a sort of immense prison, where it was not possible for me to meet someone who would give me some credit, trust, a crumb of esteem. I struggled like a large moth attracted to a treacherous light in the night, blinded by things that I still had to learn to fear. It was an ugly, wicked, male chauvinist society for sure. I realized, not through deduction, but through direct observation, that it was also a mafioso society.

All around Virzì and inside as well, grievous things would happen. Those lands were used for the secret transport of heads of livestock, cattle and sheep, the fruit of rustling committed in the province of Trapani, headed for the slaughterhouse in Palermo, going along the interior, closely watched short cuts that led to the safe junction in the hills of Monreale. What desperation! You knew the area where they began their crossing through our land and the point of arrival. You knew the animals were stolen from this owner or the other, but you had to keep your lips sealed. By not doing so, then as now, the worst can happen. I was able to get an example of the immediate punishment that could unexpectedly strike you in 1939, I believe, from the fate that befell Vincenzo L., the old field guard who had had that job for over twenty years at Presti and Virzì, our two former feudal estates. 'A highly esteemed person,' according to my grandfather's opinion, and mine, to this day. Maybe before being betrayed by an informer, Don Vincenzo was betrayed by his own abandon to an old man's pleasure of talking to himself out loud, in order to feel alive. It happened that one rainy evening he caught the distant sound of a herd plodding through thick mud, and headed outside to see which way all those animals were coming from. It was as he had imagined, based on what sign I would not know. And he said to himself, but out loud, 'Ah, Agostino's sheep ...,' as he went calmly back inside the courtyard.

It was not worth finding out who had heard him. What counted was the fact that the very next day Don Vincenzo resigned from his job as field guard. He apologized to the lady owners of the estates – my sister Caterina and me – for resigning. His attitude was deeply mortified, but at the same time, his voice was absolutely firm. After which he pulled his black visored cap clear down to his eyes, climbed on his mare, and left our lands forever.

Another example of the cruel necessity, in Mafia climates, to be careful not to give any sign of having seen or heard anything pursues me through the years with burning remorse: the encounter I had the misfortune to have unexpectedly one morning in early autumn, in the thicket of reeds where I had ventured, looking for the first wild turnips of the season. A terrifying encounter!

The murdered victim was almost a child, he couldn't have been even fifteen years old. A young shepherd, judging by his sheepskin vest. Blowflies and wasps flitted around on his chalkish face near his mouth, which gaped open with a rock stuffed in it, meaning: 'You talked, now you'll never talk again.'

I too am talking about him for the first time. After something like half a century, finally. In order to accuse myself, finally. For the unforgivable sin of not snatching that rock out of his mouth. Why didn't I do it? Why?

Up to now I have spoken about sensations and suspicions. And then about behaviours emblematizing subjection to the dictates of *omertà*. The direct clash with the Mafia was yet to come. Deeds and misdeeds that fell to me to deal with began, of course, with antecedents. It was like this. Before arriving at the frontal attack with the adversary, there were 'warnings.' Many of them, strong ones, intended to wear me down. Just as in a bullfight, it is the picadors' job to weaken the bull.

I began feeling hunted when I received increasingly frequent anonymous letters that suggested I do such and such and not do something else, that I should be very careful not to hire so and so or not to fire some other guy. Repulsive letters in themselves and disgustingly written, which I would quickly tear up. Then a letter arrived for me that was better written, and signed *lu cani e lu gaddu*,[3] much more clearly alluding to the relation between the two parties directly concerned: the dog = obedience, the addressee – me! The rooster = king of the roost, the writer – him!

The rooster proposed a meeting to the dog, at the crossroad for Gibellina, on a certain date at the hour of Ave Maria.[4] If I accepted, fine. And if not, it was understood that the appointment would be changed to the third day of threshing on the threshing floor at Virzì. Was this a matter of a real invitation to an eye-to-eye talk, a bad joke, a rudimentary offer of sexual favours? Such irritating hypotheses – they did not deserve even the least bit of attention, the slightest break in my personal ritual of casting ugly things, obstacles, and disappointments into oblivion. Or, to be more precise, the slightest break in my impulse to throw myself into the game of blindman's bluff with life. With fortune. With the unknown. With destiny.

So, yielding to the convenient saying 'We'll see,' I not only forgot about that letter, but about all the others that had come before it. One of them had advanced such a string of threats against me that it made me think they were unlikely: Vulgar, grotesque lies, boasting, and vain rantings. Nothing more. The letter in question contained the following crude spectre.

Dear Madam I warn you that if you don't come to an agreement we will proceed first of all to burn the wheat crop then to cut down the grape vines in the vineyard then to get signor Pellegrino out of the way and then we were to go further still ...

Today, in light of what we have seen follow intimidations of this kind, it is unbelievable that I split my sides with laughter at that missive before I tore it to pieces. Nevertheless, it seemed obligatory to plan a defensive move as a precautionary measure. Not for me personally, but for my children, so they would avoid some kind of punishment for my actions, which one or more wicked men might have proposed to inflict on their innocent lives. So I took pains in one of my evening conversations with the sharecroppers to drop the information, as if by chance, that in even the remotest event of some 'offence' directed at me or anyone else in my family, well then, the various names of the probable authors of the offence were kept in the care of three notaries located in three different cities in Italy. I was lying, it was a bluff. But the aim was achieved. One of the men present would certainly have told the necessary person, and he would not have made a move. At least that was what I thought. And I took a flight back to

Rome joyfully, totally forgetting about those sinister warnings, warnings about which, if my desire to be carefree had not been so strong, I would rightly have had to inform the other person exposed to capital punishment – Totò Pellegrino. But my intolerance for the very hypothesis of a punishment inflicted upon me required that I exclude any fear of revenge taken out on my administrator's back, according to the workings of evasion of a form of servitude.

The letter arrived for me before summer. It must have been May. I remember that the wheat was still green, a very promising crop for its quality and quantity.

No, I did not say anything to anyone about the anonymous threats. I would have lost face. I was the one who had received the warnings, so it was a private matter, to be settled directly with the person who had fired the warnings at me on small pieces of cheap paper. Warnings of a superior calibre, typical of the big-shot Mafia bosses.

I reacted to the suspicion of such an eventuality with more laughter and a wave of pride came over me too. Ah yes, Samson and Delilah? Fine, we'll see about that!

In July, when I returned to Virzì for the harvest, Totò Pellegrino came as always to pick me up at the Palermo airport. He looked ill, as if recovering from a bad fever. Along the road to Virzì, he answered my questions about farm business with difficulty, and when we arrived at Alcamo he forgot to suggest the usual short stop at the Caffè Siracusa, where the owner would serve me a lemon granita with his own hands, without us even ordering it first. Contrary to habit, he was driving the car slowly, so slowly that – I remember it perfectly – to my delight the bursts of cicadas rejoicing in the scorching heat reached me from the sides of the road.

It was precisely a little before noon that I saw a tall column of dark black smoke rising up behind the Sirignano hill. I said, 'There must be a fire over there.'

'Yes, there is,' replied Totò Pellegrino in a lifeless voice.

'Come on, speed up,' I ordered.

The threshing floor at Virzì was completely engulfed in flames. The entire harvest of wheat and all the bales of straw stacked up behind the threshers were burning. There wasn't a shadow of a doubt, I immediately connected the fire with the anonymous letter. Yes, yes, of course. But then and there my mind suppressed all at my defeat, intervening on the side of my atavistic haughtiness. Aren't the unconscious and nature perhaps indirectly responsible for our behaviours?

I had to forget the humiliation I had been dealt – and I forgot it, then and there, under the pressure of having to show that I was a match for my adversaries. And if not stronger than them, then possibly less cowardly. So, addressing the group of men who were there silently watching that spectacular devouring blaze, I said, 'Ashes are excellent fertilizer! If the wind doesn't blow them away before nightfall, gather them up and put them in the storeroom with the manure. God will provide ...'

Those words were supposed to mean, for everyone who was there, that I did not have any intention of taking legal action over what had happened. Which one of them could I have accused?

Here and there the sun was peeking through the first breaks in the screen of smoke when a young, clean-cut officer with a mainland accent turned up from the Sirignano Carabinieri Command. He observed the site of the fire, questioned some of the onlookers, then spoke to me, after politely moving me apart from the others into the shade of the palm tree. Not immediately, but after a long moment of almost painful concentration, he burst out in a rush:

'Signora, I know who you are. I read your novel, an important book. A book that imparts the fine mind of the person who wrote it. Therefore, I beg you, Signora, help me. Tell me, in all conscience, if you think the fire started by spontaneous combustion or was intentionally set. Don't be afraid to talk. Look at this! Read what's on this paper! You see? It's the order for my transfer back to where I'm from. To Mantova, you see? Finally. Let me leave a happy man, I beg you. Because, you know, in over three years of service in Sicily, I've never received even the slightest hint of explicit information divulged about one of the continual wrongdoings perpetrated in this area. You, Signora, are a civilized, cultivated, clearly understanding person. Tell me, for my personal satisfaction, only as a courtesy. Tell me if I'm right to believe the fire was arson.'

In my turn, I hesitated a long time before answering him, with downcast eyes, 'Spontaneous combustion, sir. Precisely that.'

He spread his arms open, let them drop to his sides like logs, and turned his back on me. Only as he got on the seat of his motorcycle did he make a sign of goodbye, stiffly giving me a military salute.

Since then, I have asked myself why I answered that way, going against the common sense of morals, and the answer is still the same today. Because at the slightest sign on my part of insubordination, the threat of the fire carried out punctually on the day and at the place indicated in the letter would shortly require making good on the second threat – cutting down the grape vines. This time the damage would have been much more serious. Not only because the re-establishment of the entire vineyard would have cost three years of expenses without any return, but most important of all because a dozen of the sharecroppers' families, who were potential half-owners of what the vineyard produced, would have been literally reduced to starvation by my own fault.

So I answered the representative of Justice: *Spontaneous combustion*. I did it, though I felt sorrow, a very sharp conflict of conscience, and mortification, which gave me a sense of malaise that still comes over me to this day.

I emerged from this experience beaten, but with a deeper knowledge of the language of silence to adhere to with the people who lived around me at Virzì. Their faces appeared fleetingly, some of them frightened, some pensive, and others completely impassive. We all certainly needed to talk about what had happened, but there were not any comments, from me or them, just furtive looks crossing, like wary animals.

Before nightfall, the ashes from the fire were swept up, the incident was closed and sealed tight. Or, to be more exact, it was buried alive, beneath a tombstone.

In the dead of night, turning to the full moon, I confided my discovery: I was not the owner of Virzì. I was simply the one who paid the taxes, who vainly pronounced that this must be done, not that. In short, I was a pathetic puppet. Someone else was wielding the command on my land; the reins of power in the entire province – and maybe beyond – were in the hands of someone who remained unnamed.

'Vincenzo Rimi? Am I right?' The moon customarily smiles upon those who ask her questions confidently. 'Him? The son of the old sheep breeder at Virzì, back when Presti, Virzì, Pigno, Marcanza, and Lattuchella were all one pasture land?'

This time the moon hid behind a cloud. Sure, it had to be Vincenzo Rimi. I know the signs of inanimate objects.

Vincenzo Rimi. This name runs throughout hundreds of pages of documents published by the Parliamentary Commission of Inquiry into the Mafia. Police reports and court sentences reconstruct the various stages of his criminal career up to the life sentence for murder handed down on him in 1969. On him and his son Filippo.

A district attorney of Trapani, providing information on Vincenzo Rimi to the commission in 1969, said, among other things, that he 'had begun his activities as an apprentice employed to watch over fifteen sheep, and at present owns property worth over half a billion lire.'[5] Lire, mind you, at their 1969 value. The district attorney added that already in 1962, Vincenzo Rimi from Alcamo and Salvatore Zizzo from Salemi had become the 'undisputed and obeyed' heads of the Mafia operating in the Trapani area. We learn from the same documents that in 1933, at the age of twenty-five, Vincenzo Rimi was sent into forced residence[6] for the first time. And that in 1942 he was in forced residence in Ustica, already rising to the top, but so poor that his wife asked for one thousand lire in government aid ...[7]

The fire that burned the entire harvest of grain heaped on the threshing floor forced me to think about the fate of my farming estate. It was no game. First, the warning in the anonymous letter, then the fulfilment of the threat promised in it were their unequivocal system for an opening to the *conversation* with me. To the *sit-down*. With me, by necessity. With a woman, for the first time in the history of the high Mafia in western Sicily, the most rigorously traditionalist of all.

The fact that I had behaved exactly like a person of utmost secrecy with the carabinieri officer must, I suppose, have given the 'rooster,' or the person acting on his part, the proof that I was a person who could be trusted. I had not accused, grumbled, or insinuated anything.

A good bit of time passed before new hints of a storm rose from the calm, like stagnant waters, with blasts of messages coming from the mouths of two or three strangers who arrived at Virzì – one on a donkey, the others in a car – with one excuse and another. The first one asked for a bottle of water, and the other ones asked to borrow a tank of gas. The overseer helped them out, but they insisted on thanking me personally, very obstinately waiting for 'Signora Livia to consent.'

I obliged them, lending an ear to their *parlatine*.[8] It was a matter of accepting the invitation to a meeting with 'the person Your Ladyship is waiting for.' I did not have any choice, I accepted the invitation from the person who remained unnamed. For better or worse I was moving towards an unprecedented event in the history of the traditional Mafia: a woman called to present herself at a council of men at the top of the most secret power of the very *mens dei*, way up there.

I have no memory of the exact date of the appointment. But it took place on a day in the height of summer for sure. As for the year, it must have been 1955, the year after the fire. Because that carabinieri officer who begged me to be frank with him told me that he had read *La vigna di uve nere*. My first novel, published, this is certain, in 1953. Therefore, in 1954 the fire, the next year, the meeting with Vincenzo Rimi. I remember the room where the meeting took place perfectly, but not the way to get there. Only one of us was told the itinerary to follow. It was almost certainly Nanà, the driver who took us to a certain spot in the country, where another car was waiting for us in the shade of a large carob tree. We got in the other car, the three of us who were authorized to come: my brother-in-law Piero Mirto, Totò Pellegrino, and me. Nanà, our driver, stayed to wait for us at the same place he had brought us. At the carob tree.

The driver of the car that had picked us up was a young, elegant man, wearing a sand-coloured, linen jacket, and a small white cloth hat instead of the usual black visored cap. I was sitting next to him, and tried to say something to him. It was as if I were talking to a mannequin posed on the other side of a shop window.

From byway to byway, we suddenly emerged on a path that lead us to an old farmhouse, surrounded by prickly pear bushes.

The young man showed us into a dimly lit room, from which we made our way up the rungs of a ladder, then through an opening in the ceiling, reaching a sort of attic loft. But maybe it was actually a real granary, because the air up there was full of fine chaff dust, so much so that I started coughing, as I do in spring because of my allergy to pollen.

At the centre of the huge empty space in that granary loft was a round table made out of a disk of poor, rough wood, placed on a stump that still had its bark. The two Rimis, the father Vincenzo and his son Filippo, were already sitting at the table. If I had not been certain that I was in western Sicily, I could have mistaken them for Anglo-Saxon gentlemen. Vincenzo Rimi had a lean body, blue eyes, an ordinary face, a silvery head of thick hair, and beautiful hands of measured movements. His son Filippo had the attractive looks of a young romantic poet, with soft black hair, a pale complexion, a melancholy expression, and lanky body. He was dressed in a silk shirt that was unbuttoned at the collar and a blue cloth jacket over tawny slacks.

Neither of the two men stood up. The father affably told us to have a seat, pointing to three chairs placed around the rough wooden disk, on which there were five small cups, with the espresso already poured and sugar added, each one set in front of the five seats. Again the father spoke, inviting us to have a sip of the coffee and to ask him for more sugar, if we wanted it. His son seemed sleepy. He did not raise his eyes from his own hands, crossed on the edge of the table.

The first one to speak was the father, naturally. Naturally is the precise thing to say, since it was not the son's place to open his mouth. Ever. The son had the role of silent witness. That is, to be present wherever his father might move his strings, there in the granary loft as everywhere, constantly acting as a sponge, absorbing what he saw done and heard said around him, with the well-calculated aim of inheriting the father's knowledge. And with it, the certainty of one day administering to his full advantage the secret power possessed by his father.

I was only able to understand this, however, a long time later, from the involvement that I was forced to have in subsequent events. On that morning, full of nervous tension, I was just being careful not to make the mistake of losing my temper, the only possible weapon of defence and, who knows, perhaps offence too, by virtue of well-placed sarcasm.

Having finished his coffee, Vincenzo Rimi started to talk. Far from the heart of the matter, he spoke in turns of phrase of no importance that went round about, just like a falcon hovering around the object of its precise predatory interest. He began with comments on the hot weather, and the disappearance of the summer showers, so good for the vineyards and olive trees, and the appearance, instead, of insects that are resistant to American DDT ... Then, still by way of allusions, he brought the monologue closer and closer to his objective:

'Yields are very low on certain properties ... things aren't going the way they should ... they're going badly ... but in this world all things can be fixed ... all things except death. All things, for those who are alive ... You just need to know how they have to be fixed ... How and why.'

Here I interrupted him. With my heart pounding madly, but speaking in a tone that was almost as impassive as his, I said, 'Signor Rimi, the how and the why as seen by one individual don't always correspond to the how and the why as seen by other people.'

He promptly answered me, 'Certainly, that's nothing new. There are far-sighted people and there are short-sighted people. But I'll take the liberty of reminding you that there is always one person who, having no need of glasses, takes the right view of things. And he gets straight to what's in his sight. How and when he wants.'

I remember I desperately searched the faces of my brother-in-law, Totò Pellegrino, and Filippo Rimi himself for help. But no one moved. They did not even blink an eye. I had no alternative. I decided to face the situation candidly, without the useless parrying of words. All in one breath I said, 'Enough of this round-about talk. Let's get to the point. What exactly do you want?'

'For you to fire, this very day, your field guard Benedetto Lombardo.'

'Why, what has he done wrong? Of all of my employees and share-croppers, he is the best person, the most honest. What do you have against him?'

'Benedetto Lombardo *'un sapi maniari 'a scupetta.'*[9]

The metaphor struck me like thunder and lightning all at once. It meant: *Benedetto doesn't know how to kill.* A terrifying pronouncement that instantaneously made it impossible to even imagine a counter-offence. But, precisely because of this, I fell back on a crafty move. I spoke to Vincenzo Rimi in the manner of normal negotiations over a minor point of contention, as I would with any ordinary adversary, using the calm voice of a mediator. Staring at the whirl of flies over our five heads, I said, 'I didn't expect this kind of proposal. It's a rather tall request on your part. And on my part such action would be uncon-scionable. You've caught me off-guard. I can't tell you yes or no. I have the grape harvest coming, and Benedetto has always been my right hand in those long days full of hard work. I need his help. And to make a decision when it's convenient for me. So, I can give you an answer a *sirratizzi arripostati.*[10] I have to have this and you must grant it.'

Then something surprising happened. With the palms of his hands spread wide open, Vincenzo Rimi gave a single blow to the top of the table, and we saw the five small coffee cups jump into the air – going up all together from the shaking, old wooden disk and falling back down with their saucers, while his voice exploded in both surprise and enjoyment, *'Minchiuni, pi' essiri 'na fimmina, buona arraggiuna!'*[11]

Encouraged by this compliment, and susceptible as I am to the pleasure of risks, I added, 'Is it clear, at the end of the grape harvest?' He answered yes with a nod of his head. But still not satisfied, I con-tinued to speak in a coquettish voice, 'But let it be very clear that beginning on the first of August, I'm coming down from Rome and planting myself at Virzì. And I'm staying there, with the door open, doing everything I please, deciding everything the way I think. Without hearing any other news arrive for me.'

The witnesses to all of this are dead, but I am not lying. The conversation went exactly as stated above, with the concluding sentence spoken to me by Vincenzo Rimi included: 'Madam, you may go to Rome, and return to Virzì when you wish. You may do things your own way until the day we agreed upon, both of us.'

And return I did, in the height of that Sicilian summer that Tomasi di Lampedusa describes with so much repulsion. I burrowed in, in the 'boundless countryside of feudal Sicily: desolate, without a breath of air, oppressed by the leaden sun.'

In accordance with the commitment made in front of Rimi, I returned precisely on the first of August. Even though I already regretted the useless boldness that brought me to suffer voluntarily from that hellish climate. But a point of honour prevented me from saying, even to myself, no, I'll arrive on the 2nd, the 10th, or the 15th, because I prefer the seashore at Capri, or because I have a stomach ache or some other stupid little things of the sort. Yes, the first of August I arrived punctually at Virzì, entirely alone in the huge living quarters, with the main door open day and night. And already the next day, I started making decisions that were entirely superfluous. Like, for example, the decision to cut down some reeds that would not have been of use to anyone that month, and to whitewash the entire perimeter of the courtyard, which was due to be cleaned again in late autumn. But I had to live up to the big talk that I had let out of my mouth concerning my right to do and undo whatever I wished, just as I liked. Everything, the way I thought, until the deadline agreed upon with Rimi.

Oppressed by the heat wave, boredom, and irritation with myself, I went on until September in the most complete isolation. The time for the grape harvest arrived at last. Every one of its rituals was carried out in perfect order right up to the last day. Then the accounts with the sharecroppers were settled. The vats, tubs, copper amphoras, and large vats for the grape must were thoroughly washed, rinsed, dried, and put back in the equipment storeroom. My seat on the airplane for Rome was guaranteed by the ticket that the administrator had gone to pick up for me in Palermo. The sun set behind the hills at its usual hour on that day, the deadline for my obligation to fire the dear, innocent Benedetto Lombardo, and the moment arrived when I waved my hand to call him over to accompany me on my evening walk down the lane of eucalyptus trees. We walked along side by side in a silence broken only by our steps thudding in the dust. It was like that up to the bend in the lane where the estate quarters disappeared from sight. I stopped there, and in a voice that was certainly different from normal, I spoke to him as if looking for help, my hands outstretched, searching for his, stammering, 'Benedetto ... Benedetto, I have to talk to you about something ...'

Benedetto moved away a step to answer in a virile voice of absolution, '*Voscenza 'un m'avi a diri nnenti. Saccio chiddu ca voscenza fici e disse a mio onore, e la ringrazio. E da 'stu momento 'un sugnu cchiù vostru campiere, torno a essiri vostro mezzadro. Taliasse, scarico ccà stesso 'a scupetta e sugnu prontu a cunsignarila a 'ccu 'a pritenni.*'[12]

He unloaded the cartridges from his weapon, threw them on the dusty lane, and drove them into the ground, heavily stomping his hobnailed boots.

Then I waited until we reached the end of the bend in the lane of eucalyptus, and there I hugged him, and he hugged me, and we stayed like that for quite a long while, one clasped to the other in the most absolute silence.

This was the end of our fellowship, an end marked by the sudden fall of night, and the leaves of the eucalyptus ruffled by the wind.

The next day, Benedetto Lombardo handed over the shotgun and his gun licence, whether to the police or the carabinieri, I wouldn't know. He went back to being an ordinary sharecropper and I went back to Rome, to my children, in the enormous, light-filled penthouse in Via Emilia, the highest spot of downtown Rome, 'within the city walls.'

The fire set to the harvest, then the firing of my trustworthy field guard ... And then what else would there be? For how long? And why? That's it, the ultimate aim of the unnamed person: to take possession of Virzì. Step by step along the main road leading to the siege of the fort. In this particular case, to wearing down my ability to resist.

The next step was the *advice* (that is to say, the imposition) to hire a certain Masi Parrino, a complete stranger to me, for Benedetto Lombardo's job. I accepted the *advice*, which was passed on to me in Rome by Totò Pellegrino. I could not have done otherwise. Because in the notorious anonymous letter, his name appeared on the third level of the rooster's steps of punishments to be carried out if I failed to submit.

I met Masi Parrino in person many months after he came to Virzì. He was a short little middle-aged man, fair-haired, restless, a Rodomonte.[13] Even without reading it on the farmhands' faces, it was immediately clear that he was a henchman, completely ignorant about farming matters. A low-level boss, but situated in a position of command to show off incessantly to my employees and me. He would give orders to the workers to do stupid tasks that they often did not perform well, catching on right away that he could not tell the difference between something that was done or just left as it was. He would brag to me about his initiatives, for example: 'I had the quinces picked before the bees sucked them' or 'I had the oil in the truck changed before the engine burned.' Such chores were never done with his own hands. He was busy smoking one cigarette after another and, naturally, by the light of the stars shooting dead centre any bird flying in the courtyard at Virzì, bats and owls included.

I heard tell from several people that Masi Parrino was a well-known murderer and, worse still, an infallible hired killer for the unnamed person, in his employ for years. Always with favourable results for the person requesting his services, even in the Courts of Justice. One person told me about an absolutely astonishing *execution*. It was more a show of infamy than an outright criminal act.

There were a lot of spectators – more or less all the notables of Alcamo, sitting around the tables at the Caffè Siracusa in the main piazza, at the usual time for their afternoon granita. They saw Masi Parrino get up from his small table together with his foster-brother, take his arm, slowly lead him beyond the maze of chairs occupied by the idle clientele, all men, of the large, open-air caffè, and calmly make his way towards the far end of the piazza, emptied by the sun's heat beating down. When he got there, with the other man kept close at his side, they saw him shoot his brother in the liver with his gun, let him fall on his back with open arms, and continue walking as if nothing had happened, continue at a steady pace, and finally turn out of the sunny piazza into a small street. There, the people sitting at the Caffè Siracusa lost sight of him, and were ready to swear there hadn't been enough time to see who the killer could be.

I heard whispers of another person who died at his hands, but never of handcuffs for him, witnesses for the prosecution, trials, or prison. Whether what reached my ears was true or not, I could not expect anyone to confirm. Was that man really a criminal, or some poor guy who was unjustly slandered? In either case, he had slipped into Virzì, and I had to keep him. But he was a thorn in my side. I could not sleep there at night. How could an individual with that kind of notorious criminal record move around freely? And in fact, he did not move around freely for long. It must have been 1960 or thereabouts, when Masi Parrino disappeared from Virzì and Alcamo. Finally suspected of various criminal activities, he was sent into forced police residence in a small town in the north. In Friuli, I think. Months passed, and I continued to pay him his salary as field guard through my administrator. It went to Alcamo, to his home, into the hands of some relative of his. Was it right to continue paying an individual who, in addition to leaving his employer in the lurch, had huge accounts pending with the Justice system – and who knows when they would be settled? My husband and one of his friends who was a lawyer also thought it was not necessary to pay him *sine die* undeserved compensation for services that he did not perform. From Rome, I explained my point of view to Totò Pellegrino over the phone, in such a state of extreme exasperation that I rebutted each time his weak yet obstinate 'It'll be hard,' 'It'll be hard' with sharp shouts: 'Hurry up! Explain yourself! Solve it!'

After my blustering stream of orders, the person on the receiving end of the rebuke did not do anything right away. By contrast, as if under the influence of a narcotic, I was overcome by obliviousness to the 'thing' that had gotten me so fired up, and beaten. It was not the effect of drugs that had always made me able to fly from painful situations to unreal paradises. It was egotism, I imagine.

I would really like to know, in the next life, if it was luck or misfortune to let myself go ahead by force of inertia in ever new gravitational orbits, or spheres of influence, whichever one might say. It doesn't matter whether they were of great or slight importance, whether useful or just pleasurable.

NOTES

1   The Pillars of Hercules boast a long history, originating in Greek mythology. According to legend, they were formed after Perseus killed Medusa and later showed her head to Atlas, who immediately became a towering mountain. The ideas about the geographic location of the Pillars of Hercules vary according to different traditions in the West and East, as well as historical periods. According to some scholars, the Greeks around 250 BC would locate the Pillars on the Strait of Sicily, but with Eratosthenes

they were moved to Gibraltar, an event raising intriguing questions that Sergio Frau investigates in *Le Colonne d'Ercole, un'inchiesta* (The Pillars of Hercules, An Inquiry) (Rome: Nur Neon, 2002). Likely most pertinent in De Stefani's text is the idea that the Pillars of Hercules marked the limit of the Western World, as expressed by Dante in *The Divine Comedy*.

2 'Here there's no need to lock the main door.'

3 'the dog and the rooster.'

4 The hour of Ave Maria is in the evening.

5 Half a billion lire: approximately half a million dollars.

6 During the Fascist regime (1922–42) and thereafter, criminals were often sent into forced, or confined, residence in small towns. Typically, northerners were sent to the south, and southerners to the north.

7 Though the equivalent of less than one dollar today, in 1942, one thousand lire would have been a fair amount. For instance, in 1940, office workers of the lower middle class earned approximately 400 lire a month, and day labourers earned around 9 lire per day on average.

   As De Stefani notes in the original, this official description of Vincenzo Rimi is drawn from passages provided to her by Marcello Cimino.

8 *parlatine*, talks using the linguistic codes or jargon of the Mafia.

9 ''un sapi maniari 'a scupetta' – 'doesn't know how to shoot a gun.'

10 'a sirratizzi arripostati' – 'when the vats are back at rest.'

11 'Good heavens, for a woman, she reasons well!'

12 'Your Ladyship doesn't have to say a thing to me. I know how much your Ladyship did and said on behalf of my honour, and I thank you. From this moment on, I'm not your field guard. I'm going back to being your sharecropper. Look, I'm unloading the gun here and I'm ready to turn it over to the person who wants it.'

13 Rodomonte, a figure in the Sicilian puppet theatre, was known as an aggressive, bragging warrior.

Testimony

MARIA SALADINO

When I was twenty-five I found out I was the daughter of a mafioso.

And my world caved in on me. Me with my Christian principles, me with my ambitious projects to eradicate violence and evil from my land, me with my dreams of defeating the Mafia, starting with the children, me of all people, I was a mafioso's daughter.

He belonged to the Mafia of a hundred years ago. A small-time bandit in the retinue of the Mafia boss of the town, my father changed his life after he got married. I never heard him voice regret about his past. And this hurt me. But he changed his life through his actions. And this consoled me. It helped me love him.

And also I knew my father had been a mafioso of the old-fashioned kind, different from the Mafia I came to know with my own eyes at the end of the 1940s, when I saw rivers of blood running through the streets of Camporeale. Terrible, just terrible. When I would walk somewhere, every street reminded me of a tragedy. There was someone killed by the Mafia every day in town. You couldn't live in peace anymore.

In those years, two Mafias hung over the town, one was about to die and the other one was about to be born. The former had a code of honour, the latter was ruthless and bloodthirsty. Both of them, in any case, were terrible. The former was headed by an old godfather. He didn't kill children and women, like they do now. But it was still the Mafia. And it sowed terror just the same. The latter had a hair trigger and wanted to rise to the top at any cost, without any mediations. Right away.

The situation in town was desperate. I taught at the elementary school; my students were so hungry they cried. I helped them the best I could. I bought them books, clothes. Bread and pasta. I was a teacher and all of my salary was spent like that.

The Mafia didn't like these things. The poor had to stay poor and needy. Always. The mafiosi had to be the only ones to help them. Their help was never disinterested. It was aimed at obtaining complicity, or conniving schemes. There wasn't room for anyone in the middle. And if a teacher like me started to comfort these people by opening the poor wretches' eyes, it was a problem. It had to be put to a stop.

I was very young when I started teaching, right after I got my diploma. My first job was in Grisì, a small town near Palermo. I met my first and only love there. He was a teacher like me. I liked his big eyes, his arms full of muscles, his round, good face. I was happy. I thought I would marry him.

But one night, Saint Rosalia appeared to me in a dream and said, 'Maria, leave this fiancé, God does not want this. If you marry, you're going against God's will.'

And I asked her, 'Are you Saint Rosalia or are you the devil?'

She answered, 'I'm Saint Rosalia and God has sent me.'

I woke up and thought, 'And what if it really was Saint Rosalia?' So I lost my peaceful-heartedness and broke off the engagement with the teacher. He was so disappointed he left to fight in the war as a volunteer. I prayed to Saint Rosalia to not let him die because my heart would feel remorse forever.

So I threw myself body and soul into my work, into teaching. When I saw all of that blood running through the streets of Camporeale I thought that something had to be done for the little children. Now I was free of emotional commitments and could roll up my sleeves. I started to teach catechism and Sunday school. I taught school in the morning and dedicated the afternoons to the children. I let them play in the courtyard near the church.

In the same piazza there was Donna Sofia's balcony. She was a bossy, complaining old woman. Every time the soccer ball landed on her balcony she loved cutting it up with a knife. But I didn't get discouraged, and without saying a word I'd buy another one right away. In one year I bought fifty soccer balls. Donna Sofia finally got tired of it and we kept on playing in peace. It was a wonderful lesson for the children. I'd showed them that you fight bullies with the weapons of civility and patience. I tried to teach them that way to be good, beautiful, and honest.

I wanted to do an apostolate[1] at Camporeale to redeem my town from the Mafia. But in 1940 it was difficult for a woman in Sicily to dedicate herself to social services. So I decided to be a missionary. I left for Grottaferrata, to stay with the Franciscan Sisters of Maria. After a few months I was supposed to go to India. But a few weeks were all it took to convince me that that wasn't the life for me. The convent's rules were too strict.

So I returned to Camporeale. I cried a lot. I asked myself what God wanted from me. To be engaged, no. To be a nun, no. Now I understand what God wanted and still wants from me. My mission is to save the children from street violence. That's how the first social centre was born.

I made up my mind right after the murder of Camporeale's mayor, Pasquale Almerico, killed on 25 April 1957. He was my best friend. A good man. He paid with his life for his opposition to the predominance of the agrarian Mafia. Together we had planned the creation of a youth village, an oasis of peace to get the small children in the Belice Valley away from the violence. Then Almerico was killed, and I continued the project.

The first thing I needed was land where the social centres could be built. And it would take an awful lot of money to buy it. I went to look for it in America. In a year and a half I had collected the funds necessary for purchasing the land. So many Italian American artists offered me their help. They would do charity events in the evening, and people paid twenty-five dollars. Half of it went to pay for the event and half went to me.

In December of 1962 I returned to Camporeale. There were fourteen million lire[2] in my purse. I started the negotiations to purchase the land, and it was an adventure. My fellow townspeople knew, in fact, that the land would be used for social works and so they kept raising the price every day. It took twenty years before my first institute was built. Twenty years of battles with everyone. An iron fist directed against the Mafia, politics, and the bureaucracy. Different forces coming together with the sole aim of wearing me down, making me give up.

But they hadn't counted on my stubbornness. In the end I won. I was able to resist them. I didn't bend. Up to now I've completed nine institutes.

The stories living in these walls are unspeakable. The acts of violence and torture these children have suffered are beyond imagination. Little children who saw their father die right beside them, riddled with bullets from machine-gun fire. In some cases, their fathers have AIDS and their mothers are in prison. Some of the other children were forced into prostitution when they were eight or ten years old. Or made to become drug dealers. There are sweet little girls, raped by their fathers, sold by their mothers. Little children who've lived in the middle of problems with alcoholism, cocaine. Poor children, abandoned by their parents with nothing to eat. The mothers of two of our children are staying at Biagio Conte, the institute that gathers up the homeless people at the central train station in Palermo. Then there's illiteracy, abject poverty.

But we manage to save a lot of them. There's a boy with family problems. I welcomed him six years ago and said to him, 'Giuseppe, I saw you have an excellent grade average at school. Do you want to study?' He answered yes. So I had him enrol at the technical institute for land surveyors and he passed with a very high grade, 50. Now he does my building construction plans, prepares my billing statements, and makes the payments to the National Institute of Social Insurance. He's my right arm. If I'd found him sooner he would have lightened a lot of my work.

Certainly there are also some failures. When they take drugs, for example. You can't do anything. They change. They lie, steal, betray the trust of their parents, their best friend. No, when it's drugs, I give up.

My mother always told me that the mafiosi didn't kill me because I'm a woman. I had clashes with the high Mafia of Camporeale and Alcamo over buying land. But I always won. They had it in for me because I wanted to buy the land where I later built the Don Bosco centre. I had to fight it out with those mafiosi, but I won. *Pigghiai pi fissa a tutti.*[3]

The women in this area are passive. They always bow their heads. When one of them rebels, like I did, the men are afraid, they're taken by surprise. They end up confused, and give in.

The mafiosi's children are different from their fathers. As long as they're in my institutes they're lambs, they tremble, they're shy, afraid. It's in their own environment that they become wild animals. But if we give them a good upbringing, if we help them to grow in a garden of hope, we transform them, tame them. The important thing is not to forget to water this garden with good feelings and good examples.

Children are not born bad, they're born good. It's their environment's fault that they come to a bad end. Compared to thirty years ago, their problems have also changed. Before, they were simply starving to death. That was the beginning of all their problems. There wasn't a crumb to eat at home and the father would steal, the mother become a prostitute.

Now, instead, there's drugs, and the ambition to be on top, even in children's hearts. The race to outdo oneself, to have the best clothes, the best cars. People don't bear with things anymore like they used to. Before, when they were poor, with a dish of pasta and cabbage they kept going, with no trouble. Now they're never satisfied with what they have.

My medicine is work. Without work there is no recuperation. That's why I created artisan woodworking shops, ceramics studios, and typography shops.

And then some of the children study. For example, there've been so many girls that have earned their diplomas with the nuns. With the help of the nuns and the Salesians[4] I hope to open more shops to provide work. Because that way everyone can be saved. Work and love. That's the medicine.

I always dream. I'm a dreamer. I dream of really beautiful things. Children freed from hunger and violence, truer social justice, a society that's not dominated by tyrants, free of the Mafia. I also dream of more youth care centres, the widespread involvement of volunteers, a city for unfortunate children. I don't know how many years I need in order to bring about all these things. My father died at ninety-seven, my mother at eighty-nine. I just need to make it to ninety in order to complete all my projects.

I thank God for having given me the heart of a child, always full of wonder, enthusiasm, joy. There are moments of sadness, when I go entire nights without sleeping, with so many troubles, so much suffering. Sometimes I suffer from insomnia and anemia, and I keep on going like an automaton, light-headed and legs unsteady. But in my heart I'm always twenty years old.

Helping others keeps you young.

NOTES

1 A mission dedicated to the propagation of religion or social work.
2 Fourteen million lire was approximately seven thousand dollars.
3 *Pigghiai pi fissa a tutti*, Sicilian dialect meaning 'I played everyone for a fool.'
4 The Salesians are members of the Society of St Francis de Sales and are devoted primarily to education.

Testimony

FELICIA IMPASTATO

It was raining the day they killed my son.

We were supposed to see each other the night before at the home of one of my cousins who was coming back from America. But Peppino never made it to that appointment. These bastards took him somewhere by force before they killed him. It must not have been hard to catch him, because he only drove on out-of-the-way roads. He didn't have a driver's licence and was afraid of being stopped by the carabinieri.

When I found out what had happened to Peppino, I felt my house cave in on me. I got a knot in my heart. I was able to scream 'Aaaaaah!' Then nothing else. I didn't talk for two days. What a horrible thing they did to him. And they didn't even let me see my dead son because he was in pieces. They thought I'd have a stroke. All they picked up on the train tracks were his hands and feet.

And I would have been satisfied just to see even these poor remains of my Peppino. I would have stroked them, kissed them. Touching his thumb would have been enough for me to feel him beside me for the last time. And instead, they didn't let me see him.

I couldn't sleep. I was afraid for my other son. They didn't leave me in peace even after they killed him. They kept telling me to be careful. Not to say anything. To resign myself.

I started to be afraid for Peppino after his father died. I was afraid that my husband's death might give the killers a free hand. They had held back up to then because of the embarrassment of having to kill the son of a friend. A son renounced, disgraceful, but the son of a friend nevertheless.

My son was an intelligent boy. And in our part of the country this is a fault, because whoever thinks with their own head is looked down upon.

He was involved in politics. And he wasn't a Christian Democrat. He had conflicts with my husband, who didn't want him to fight against the Mafia. My husband was a relative of mafiosi, so he was a mafioso. My husband always got angry with Peppino because he criticized the Cinisi mafiosi. As soon as he heard him say the word Mafia, he'd fly into a rage. He'd grab him by his shirt collar and throw him against the wall. But he didn't give him any satisfaction. He'd stare him straight in the eyes and walk out of the house. He'd come back at night, when he was sure he wouldn't see his father.

Peppino was a good, serious, polite boy. He fought against the Mafia. And twenty years ago this was a fault. Then he opened up the music and culture centre and he brought along all the young people who were kind of misfits. He wanted to salvage them, get them out of the Mafia's grips. They didn't do anything bad, they watched films, listened to music. He was magnetic.

When he was about eighteen he'd started to be involved in politics. He was a communist, a member of the Proletarian Democracy Party. I was scared, I told him to stop. Because the Mafia doesn't forgive anyone. And he'd say, stroking my hair, 'Mama, these kids need to understand.' He told them about the evils of the Mafia. And he was right.

So many times I tried to make my husband understand. But every time I talked about Peppino he got angry. He'd yell and go off to the men's club. And when he came back he'd tell me, 'If you speak about that person again I'll throw you out of the house.'

My son wouldn't bend for anyone, he was a fighter. He'd say to me, 'Mama, the people of Cinisi accept the Mafia as if it were a necessary evil. And the trouble is that even with the proof right in front of them, they refuse to renounce it. And papa, it must be clear, is one of them.' Peppino fought for the good of his town, which, ungrateful as it was, in return showered him with insults because everyone here was on the Mafia's side. For everyone the Mafia meant work and protection.

Now, instead, they say it would be good to have who knows how many more like him. Now he's a sort of hero here. But when he was alive no one defended him. They said, 'He was opposing the town's economic development.'

I didn't care at all about what they said in town. My son had good ideals. That was enough for me. I gave him protection. I let him come in the house in secret, I gave him something to eat, let him wash, prepared what he needed, and then helped him get away as soon as I heard his father arriving. Father and son never saw each other during these escapes. I think though that my husband knew I was helping him. He pretended not to notice. After all, he was his own blood.

After the tragedy with Peppino, I found out from the carabinieri that before my husband died he had been in America. He hadn't told me anything about it. I think the Italian American Mafia, feeling attacked by my poor son, invited him to offer some guarantees about Peppino. He had to reassure them that he would convince his son to stop it all. And I don't believe the Mafia heard my husband say what they expected. Besides, father and son hadn't had any kind of relationship for a while. I imagine these bastards in front of my husband. I hear them speaking. Pounding their fists on the table. And he's like stone. Silent. Impotent.

On that terrible rainy day when the carabinieri came to my home I thought there'd been some kind of fight. I asked what had happened and they answered it was kid stuff. But they looked for photos. So I asked, 'Did they kill my son?' They said, 'Signora, calm down, nothing's happened.'

The police detectives immediately followed two lines of investigation. A failed act of terrorism and suicide, excluding homicide for no reason. But I didn't believe it. I knew they had killed him. Peppino had received threats. I felt inside that they would kill him in the end. Everyone in town thought that.

After his death I didn't keep quiet, I did something. I didn't want my son to pass for a suicide or a terrorist. There was no one in town, not even among his detractors, willing to support the suicide theory. Even though they didn't say it openly in the beginning, the townspeople in Cinisi were all convinced that Peppino had been killed by the Mafia.

Not to mention the theory about an act of terrorism. No one could imagine Peppino holding a bomb ready to blow up a section of train tracks. Everybody knew my son was non-violent.

After his death, what hurt me the most was the investigators' silence. There was so much resistance to recognizing Mafia murders because the magistrature back then was at the service of a corrupt, mafioso political class.

In the beginning, I wanted to keep quiet. I was petrified with fear. I decided to talk when I understood that my silence was drowned out by the talk spread by people who had an interest in making my son pass for being crazy or a terrorist. I raised my voice above all the others and for the first time I became authoritative. The authority who gives the dignity of pain. And from that moment on I have never stopped. I've talked to defend my son's memory and I'll defend it forever.

I'm old, what can they do to me. If they kill me they still can't take away the freedom my son gave to me with his death. The freedom not to be afraid, the freedom to have said 'the Mafia is disgusting' when no one was saying it. By now I don't care about anything in my life anymore. They already took away my greatest love.

Minister of the Interior Gava wanted me to give him proof that my son had been killed by the Mafia. I replied that the investigators had to look for it, if they had the courage. All they had to do was to start from one fact: my son attacked the Mafia in a town governed by the Mafia. And even the children in our area know that this kind of attitude in the 1970s amounted to a death sentence.

It took Caponnetto's[1] opinion to establish definitively the Mafia matrix of the killing. It was an important event for me. The contribution made by Chinnici[2], who conducted the judicial inquiry and with whom I talked, was also valuable.

I also talked with Borsellino,[3] who asked me how I could affirm it was the Mafia who killed my son. I answered with a simile. 'Honorable Judge,' I said, 'at school the teachers give orders and the students obey. It's the same in the Mafia. The leaders give orders and the young men carry them out.'

The orders came from far away, the hired killers came from nearby. And so they did what they had to do to my son.

Since my son's murder, my life has changed a lot. I find the strength to go on living only by looking at his photograph. He has a deep look on his face that has remained inside me. This photograph isn't hanging on the wall. The nail is inside my heart. It bleeds and keeps me company. It bleeds because this son of mine still has not had justice.

After so much time, Peppino's killers have no face. The day they catch them I won't even want to look them in the face because they disgust me. And I wouldn't even want to take revenge because I've never liked that. But I would like to know they're in prison. I would really like that.

But at this point I don't believe in justice anymore. Even though I wish justice would be done. That they'd be punished for what they did.

Through all these years I've tried to get used to the pain. I've learned to have respect for it. It keeps me company. Certainly I still have anger inside and so many other things. Anger for the contempt shown by his father's relatives. Not one of them stayed by me. They're still convinced Peppino was kind of looking for what he got.

I have two little grandchildren, a little boy and a little girl. Both of them have always been curious about my black clothes. But how can you explain mourning to two small children? You can't. There aren't any words. It was hard to talk to them about Peppino when they were little.

When the little girl started to read, she found a poster in my papers, which said, 'The Mafia kills and silence does too.' She went to my daughter-in-law to ask what those words meant. Her mama didn't know what to tell her, what to explain. And she came to ask me. 'When people are afraid they don't say what they think, and become mean, deceitful. That's why,' I told her, 'you must never be afraid.'

Then the little boy, who found out from his father that his uncle Peppino had been killed by bad men, asked me if Giuseppe was rich and if that's why they killed him. I told him Giuseppe wasn't rich with money, but was rich with courage. He was a politician who criticized the Mafia when no one spoke about it because they were afraid to. And the bad men were the mafiosi. Then he said, 'Did they kill him like Borsellino and Falcone?'

Certainly, I answered, they did different things, but their death was the same. All three of them fought against the Mafia.

All three of them fought too many enemies all alone.

NOTES

1 Judge Antonio Caponetto became a famous antimafia prosecutor, and
   formed the highly effective antimafia pool, uniting magistrates who
   worked exclusively on Mafia cases.
2 Magistrate Rocco Chinnici headed the investigative office in Palermo,
   and was known for his tenacious antimafia position. On 31 July 1983,
   Chinnici and two bodyguards were murdered, with a car bomb.

3 Judge Paolo Borsellino devoted his life's work to the investigation and
   prosecution of Mafia crimes. Along with Judge Giovanni Falcone,
   Borsellino prosecuted over 500 mafiosi in the maxi-trials of the 1980s.
   After assassinating Falcone, his wife, and three bodyguards in a massive
   explosion on 23 May 1992, the Mafia killed Borsellino and five bodyguards in another catastrophic explosion on 19 July 1992.

Testimony

LETIZIA BATTAGLIA

I remember a little old woman who used to come to bring us eggs.

She'd climb the stairs up to the third floor, and when she was tired she'd stop and pee on the stairs. She wasn't ashamed. She didn't even turn around to see if there was someone watching her. She was tired and had to pee. This is a sweet memory, strangely sweet. I can still smell the strange odour of pee, disinfectant, and chicken coop. I see her from above, small and stooped over, lift her long black skirt up in a bundle, squat down and pee.

It's a memory, but it's also a photograph memory, a smell. This is the first image that comes to my mind when I think of Palermo. An image with no shame, just like this city. And even now, if I think of a snapshot capable of synthesizing the realities of Palermo, I think of a woman.

I photograph women rather a lot; they come out better for me. I satisfy an intuition that pushes me to photograph women more than men. I live this intuition like a meeting of energies. My energy instinctively meets the energy of the women I photograph.

I spent my early childhood away from Palermo, in Naples, Civitavecchia, and Trieste. When I returned to Palermo I was eleven, and I suffered a lot. My parents had decided to take away all the freedoms I had. In Trieste, at ten years old, I rode my bike around alone. When I arrived in Palermo, it wasn't possible anymore because the rhythm of women's lives was different here. It wasn't right to walk in the streets after a certain hour. It wasn't right to be out in public with boys. It wasn't right to get too familiar with outsiders. Too many things weren't right for women to do.

But I didn't pay much mind to all that. Back then I already did what I thought was right. I've always been an anti-conformist. Conformism made me suffer a lot. Times have changed now, but in the 1960s all that counted in Sicily was what other people said. Whispers and murmurs persecuted me the entire time I was growing up.

In Palermo I was sure I would never be a housewife. The city piqued my curiosity, pushed me to go outside my house. I felt the need to live in close contact with the city in order to understand its moods. Palermo fascinated me. I felt it was inevitable that I would fall in love with it. But before yielding entirely, I wanted to study it well. And the easiest way to do that was to start discovering what was happening every day in its streets, in its homes.

So I started to write for the newspaper *L'Ora*, more taken with the city than the profession of journalism. Then I realized that if the written text was accompanied with photographs the finished work was better. And I became a photographer. I wrote the articles and photographed the people I interviewed. And I ended up falling more in love with photography than writing. It's a great love that has taken up my whole life, born a little for fun and a little by necessity. And a little by chance, like the beginning of all the great love stories.

For *L'Ora* newspaper, I reported on all sorts of news, ranging from beauty contests to sports. I photographed soccer matches when it was fairly strange to see a woman on the sidelines. And then I was a news reporter during Palermo's most terrible years, the hardest years, when no one expected yet that the Mafia would dare go so far: killing a chief of police, a judge, a baby, killing journalists. First it happened to Judge Scaglione, the murder of an excellent cadaver.

In 1974, as soon as I returned from Milan, where I was living, a terrible Mafia war broke out in Palermo that started with the murder of Colonel Russo and then the secretary of the Christian Democrat Party, Michele Reina, and then Boris Giuliano. I didn't expect it, I didn't expect to see so much blood. I was proud of working as a photojournalist. I felt it was an adventurous job, full of emotions, unexpected events, encounters. A restless job for restless people like me.

But what was happening was too much, it was really humanly unbearable. Sometimes I would rush from one city to another to photograph people who'd been murdered. Photographing a trial was also very hard for me. A man in handcuffs or behind bars had to be captured in an image and this frightened me. In any case, it was the fruit of a sick, wrong society.

I was out of my mind, crazy with anger at seeing Boris Giuliano, a good police officer – finally we had a good police officer in Palermo –

lying in a pool of blood. And we didn't photograph him; they didn't let us photograph him. And it was a good thing. Seeing him there in the small corner, near the cash register in the Café Lux on the floor, was too great a pain. I was astonished, I was really angry.

When they killed Judge Chinnici I didn't go out of the house. It was eight in the morning when *L'Ora* newspaper called, and the editor told me to rush right away because something very serious had happened. And he added, 'The are five people killed.' I said no, I'm not going to photograph these dead people. I don't want to do it. I couldn't do it. I didn't want to do it. My conscience and my stomach refused to do it. I didn't go, I didn't see Chinnici lying there in pieces.

Now I don't have much time for photography anymore, but I continue to work in photography, in the sense that if someone makes a request, I print it, I'm in the dark room. What I feel I'll do soon won't involve news anymore. I want to tell my own story through the life of this city or other cities too. Nobody says I only want to photograph Palermo, but I certainly want to transmit positive energy, I would like to draw strength out of the photographs. And I think I can find it in women. Yes, this hope which is strength and is a positive energy – I will look for it among women.

I'm bewitched by Sicily. The easiest thing to do would have been to go away. And God only knows how many occasions I had to abandon it. But I feel like something really holds me here. It's the land that attracts me, it's the sky, it's the sun, it's the possibility to return to being what we once were, a cultured people, a people who respected its land, its foundations. I'm attracted by the possibility of rebuilding, of working with these people, my people.

I can't stay away from Palermo for more than ten days, even if I'm on vacation. I go to New York, or even farther away, and I have to come back after ten days. That's the limit. I can't stay away any longer than that. I often travel back and forth from Palermo around the world. I often remain in its reality. Because even when I go away, Palermo remains inside me.

I can't use very complicated cameras, I'm not fond of them. My photographs come out well even though I know very few technical things and always use a small wide-angle lens. I don't use telephoto lenses, I don't want to. I have a very basic relationship with the camera, which has become almost like a hand. I don't want a lot of electronic things. If I have a camera that focuses automatically, my photograph comes out out of focus. It comes out better when I do it myself. I take photographs more with my mind and heart than with technique.

And you have to be quick, you have to participate. I don't believe you have to be detached, I get deep inside things. For example, I remember when Franco Zecchin and I would go to take the same photograph. Mine would be tragic, and his would be something ironic. And it was the same situation. One time we went to photograph a woman alcoholic. He drew out the moment when there was something funny going on around this woman, some children playing. Instead, I took a photograph in which she has a tear on her face.

I photograph tragedy even though I don't like tragedies. I'm a woman who loves life and would like life to be happiness for everyone. I get very angry when I see some kinds of happiness built on the unhappiness of others. In my photographs, I represent the former with irony and disdain, and the latter with tension and uneasiness.

I owe the greatest satisfaction in my life to photography. I won the most important award in the world, in New York, the Eugene Smith. It was a milestone because I'll always be in the history of photography. And also because this award was given to me precisely for my work in Sicily. It's a recognition after years and years of hard work, when there was no gratification, only pain and reproaches. Police, victims' relatives, judges, everyone spitting in my face.

There was a time when photographers in Palermo were considered people to avoid. To the police, they were criminals, and for criminals, the police. The Eugene Smith award restored my dignity. And at the same time, through the affirmation of my professionalism, it rewarded an entire group, restoring it in everyone's eyes.

Then there are other satisfactions, smaller but no less important. When I go back home, I develop the negatives and feel that I have perhaps realized a dream, that there was a look, something in the middle of confusion that I was able to catch. And I felt that I was in harmony with that person, who may be a little girl, an old woman. I develop the film, make the proof, print it, and discover I've made a good photo. I feel I've added another small stone, that this thing will remain to tell the story of an epoch.

Then one day I decided to become involved in politics. I was city councillor of Palermo and a regional deputy. I was convinced that photography alone wasn't enough to denounce the deterioration of this city. It was necessary to add stronger things in order to make people understand where we were going. However, it was a sad, painful experience. I don't like politics. I'm not at ease, I don't feel happy in politics. In my opinion, politics is done in an old-fashioned way. There's too much hate, too much rancor, too much jealousy. I don't like this world of politics, which, in reality, is the mirror of the society we live in. The profiteers and turncoats pull the strings of a system made for themselves. There's no room for the idealists, for the pure.

I even comprehend the Mafia, I understand it. But I'm much more angry with the politicians of this land, who allowed people who could have been normal to become mafiosi, Mafia soldiers. Because they were pushed by politics into becoming mafiosi. When power is corrupt, you play with power and understand that in order to get things you have to be corrupt.

I'm sad for the people in the Mafia. I think they are the prisoners of rules, prisoners of false myths, of pagan gods that are money, naturally, but are also certain rules within society. And politics has legitimized these principles, making them their own. Before, the mafiosi supported the politicians to manage the contracts for public works, to have protection. Then the mafiosi didn't trust them anymore and they became politicians themselves.

In the middle of all this confusion it's difficult to distinguish justice and truth. Power is a masculine way of thinking, into which women have also fallen. I used to believe that women couldn't be inside the Mafia. Instead, today, I understand that they're in it up to their necks. Their role is to keep quiet.

Some women are talking now; they collaborate with the justice system. But they always do it to avenge a son, a lover, or a husband. They're not able to kill and they take their revenge this way, by accusing people. And if they don't hold a gun in their hands, it's not for lack of courage, it's the rules that say men have to be the ones who shoot.

Every time I pass in front of the Ucciardone prison, I have a deep sense of pain, because I think that murderers, criminals, drug dealers, everything, are there inside. But I think that if one of the men had found work, justice, something different would certainly have happened in his life. A lot of men joined the Mafia because they didn't have other options. Children who didn't find different games than guns, blackmail, drugs. Than silence.

I'm attracted by the silences that scream out, by the speechless uproar, by the stillness that suddenly emerges in the middle of rebellions. It's a silence that screams in silence. I would like instead to look for a kind of peace that is something different from silence. Not a peace born of resignation, but a peace that has been won. Instead, I'm forced to photograph harsh images that disturb. In a troubled land like this, there is silence but almost never peace.

Sicily disturbs and makes you angry. In silence. But never in peace.

Testimony

RITA ATRIA

Dear Diary ...

Partanna, 12 November 1991
It's four in the afternoon. Just now, while I was outside hanging the clothes up to dry I saw Claudio Cantalicio pass by my house in his car. It's not the first time I've seen him. Four days ago, on Saturday, November 9, I saw him pass by another time in the white car, with another person. I didn't see who the other person was because he was driving and from where I was it was impossible to see him. But I can positively say that while Claudio lowered his head, the other person moved to get a look at me. It all happened in a fraction of a second and I didn't have time to recognize him. No one but me can imagine how powerful the Accardos are. Better to stay in a cage of hungry lions than to face the Accardos' hate. I could go away to the tiniest hole in the world and crawl inside forever, but if they wanted to they would find me and kill me. It doesn't matter to me, by now they've taken away everything I had in the world. What frightens me is that it's not the first time I've seen Claudio pass by my house in the last two months. Fifteen days ago I saw Claudio with a certain Nicola, talking to each, and when those two meet out in the open in front of everyone, it means they're plotting something. For my sake, I hope it's not my funeral.

Partanna, 16 November 1991
I called Signora Annina[1] to tell her that the Partanna carabinieri asked too many questions about Nicola selling drugs. They asked his friends and acquaintances questions, about who might have supplied the heroin and who might have bought it from him. I'm afraid that in a

little while my friends – if they can be called that – won't say hello to me anymore. It's already happening.

Partanna, 20 November 1991

One in the morning and I can't sleep. I'm really worried and for the first time since Nicola's death I'm really afraid, not for me, but for my mother. The reason is, tonight at about 11:35, I heard someone knocking at our door. My mother and I were awake, but all the lights were out. My mother, after they kept on knocking persistently, asked who was there, and a voice answered that it was Andrea and he'd come to pay a visit. My mother didn't recognize him and asked him to go away, but he kept insisting. But I recognized the voice right away, as soon as I heard him speak. It was Andrea D'Anna, the young man my father had working with him in the country, and who went with him in the fields on the day he was killed. Andrea kept insisting, saying he wanted to come inside. But after my mother told him several times to leave because it was late, he finally decided to go and headed towards the lane in front of my house that leads to the street before ours, Via Manzoni. Shortly afterwards, I heard the sound of a car driving away. I told my mother who it was, because she still didn't understand. Andrea hadn't come to my house for over five years. But what I'm sure about is that he came to kill me, because I know the friendships he has with members of the Accardo clan. I know full well that he always carries a gun with him and that since he stopped working for us, he hires himself out to do the dirtiest, most illegal jobs that exist. Every morning that I took the bus, I ran into Massimo, his brother, who also does anything at all to make some money, and I realized that for almost two weeks it's been a regular thing. This morning I didn't go to school because I had to gather olives and I truly believe that it was lucky for me. If I had left to go to school this morning, I'm almost certain they would have killed me. Too many coincidences. My suspicions come from so many things. One is that Massimo has contacts with the people who own the supermarket. I already told the judges, there are people there who conduct illegal activities that are tied to the Mafia. The fact that a big drunk like Massimo would be working for those people most of all is too strange. I know all about Andrea's record, another big drunk too. But most important, he's capable, like his brother, of pointing a gun at your head without giving it a second thought. But tonight Andrea wasn't drunk, he was capable of doing what the Accardos ordered him to do through their little soldiers, which is to kill me and my mother. He was too politely insistent. I told my mother everything was okay, and made up excuses to reassure her, but I'm really afraid they'll kill me tomorrow. I hope my fears are groundless, but if not, I hope they don't hurt my mother, my fear is for her, I can't leave her in trouble. Tomorrow I'll inform the police sergeant, but first I have to make sure my mother is safe. I hope this isn't the last time I write in this notebook.

Rome, 21 December 1991
I'm starting to write again because you can never be too careful. What I want after my death is a funeral with very few people. My sister-in-law and her family should be there. My sister Anna Maria and the entire corps of carabinieri who want to be there, all the people who helped me obtain justice for the deaths of my father and brother. My mother must not come to my funeral or see me after my death for any reason. Among my uncles, only Alessio Atria can be at my funeral and no one else. It has to be a funeral with lots of flowers but I don't want white flowers. The coffin will be black or white and just a single rose must be placed on top of the coffin. My clothes must be black, preferably a jacket and pants with a black bow tie, my hair must hang loose. When they carry my coffin into the church the organ must play Schubert's Ave Maria. These are my wishes and I hope with all my heart that they'll be granted. I'm sure I won't have a long life, whether I'm killed by the people that I'll accuse during the trial or because of a promise with destiny. I'd be happy if I could live together with Nicola and my father. I hope that one day Vita Maria will learn to love her father even though she won't remember him very much. I miss my Nicola so much.

12 January 1992
It's almost nine at night, I'm sad and demoralized, perhaps because I can't dream anymore, in my eyes I see so much darkness and so much blackness. I'm not worried by the fact that I will have to die but that I will never be able to be loved by anyone. I will never be able to be happy and realize my dreams. I wish so much that I could have Nicola here beside me, to be able to feel his loving touch, I need him so much, but the only thing I can do is cry. No one will ever be able to understand the emptiness inside me, that immeasurable emptiness that everyone, little by little, has made even greater. I don't have anything anymore, all I have are crumbs. I can't tell good from bad, everything

is so dark and gloomy by now. I thought that time could heal all wounds, but no, time opens them up more and more until it kills you, slowly. When will this nightmare end?

Rome, 1992
I never wanted much in life. I always asked for little and always for what costs less, because wanting something is always so easy ... but getting even just a little love, even just a little serenity is like having to climb out of a well using only your hands, a part of your body, because the rest of it is left at the bottom, a bottom that will never have a beginning or an end.

Rome, 1992
You know, I'm writing a book, and I had Angelo and Michele Santoro read it, both of them assured me that when it's done they'll help me publish it. I'm happy about it, but I'm also worried because I ask myself if I'll ever be able to finish it, because it's not every day that I can write. In order to write I need some peace and you really know that in my life peace is a taboo, something too impossible.

Rome, 1992
Who knows why you never have enough love. Who knows why now and then the sea is so blue and calm but other times it makes its waters leap so high until they cry out and howl like some kind of call, as if it were expressing all of its rage and its pain. But you just need to speak to the sea gently and for the first time he will be the one to listen to you. When he has heard what you want to tell him, he'll rock you in his gentle waves, carry you into his most profound depths, and let you experience his most hidden beauties until you're so enchanted by that world that you'll be the one to ask him to be able to live there.

Rome, 1992
Woman would I be if I were really woman: What detail differentiates me and a woman? Maybe I haven't experienced the pleasures of the flesh yet? I didn't realize how important that could be. Maybe I'm not old enough to be a woman. Maybe I don't have the ideas and her ambitions. If this is the only thing that makes me different from her, then take me into the middle of an audience, lay me out on a bed and only then will you all understand how old I am. I'm younger than you could know, but I'll give you such immense pleasures that your soul

will delight in them more than you could dream. And if an adjective greater than that woman exists, fine, that adjective will be mine.

Rome, 1992
It's incomprehensible how a smile could fascinate you, how two eyes could make you fall in love, how a silence could make you feel bad, how a caress could make you quiver, how a voice could invade your heart, how a man's desire could reawaken your senses ... The incomprehensible, inexplicable, perhaps too many questions for one who is still just a little girl.

Rome, 1992
I really believe that Culicchia[2] will never go to jail. He killed, robbed, swindled but no one will ever be able to find the proof that indicts him and proves I'm telling the truth. I'm sure I'll never be able to make the judges believe me. I wish papa were here, he would be able to find the proof that would show him for what he really is, that is, Culicchia is just a murdering thief. But naturally the words of a seventeen-year-old girl aren't worth anything. I'm just a little girl who wants justice done and he's a man who plays the role of the good, honest, Honourable Member of Parliament to a tee. I won't be able to live anymore. But he'll continue to steal, and to hide that he was the one who had Stefano Nastasi killed. Once again, as always, the one who's best at cheating life wins.

Rome, 1992
A lie is just a beautiful, made-up woman. It's like a girl in high heels, like brown hair dyed blond, fake fingernails, a pair of pants that cover up legs. In short, a lie is like a beautiful woman in all respects, the sole difference is that it takes time to uncover lies, but women are uncovered right away.

Rome, 1992
It is night and in the sky there is only silence
and immense darkness
the city around me is still awake
and full of lights
I listen but don't hear
That city is too distant from me
or perhaps I from her

Whichever it may be, not knowing
what city is mine only makes me understand
how sweet is the pain
that ties us to its memories.

Rome, 1992
To wait for whom. Or what?
Perhaps a hope
the illusion of changing what surrounds you
so complicated because you know
what was stolen from you can never be returned
You can scream, cry, suffer,
but no one will listen, no one will understand you
instead they will judge you.

Rome, 1992
Only with time will you understand
only with water will you purify yourself
only with a mantle will you cover yourself
but with the passing of days and nights
how and from what will you protect yourself?
Perhaps from great disappointments
from great suffering
perhaps from the nos said to people
from the looks that accuse you
for what you believe is right.
Perhaps from the pure, sincere love you think you see.
No, nothing will protect you from your fears
nothing will protect you from a world that will never be yours.

Rome, 1992
A sliver of deep darkness invades you, but this time it isn't fear that
prevents you from seeing. It's actually the night, it's the dim light of
the moon that makes you wane.
    Ever so slowly, sweetly, almost making you die inside.

Rome, 1992
It's a long night and there are millions of stars in the sky, one more
enchanting than the other. In each one of them there's a little secret,
each one has a long journey to make. One of them, precisely the small-
est, the brightest, the farthest away, is making the slowest and longest

trip of all for me, in order to reach a place called infinity. That is right where my two great loves are. Right there in infinity, I'll be able to embrace my stars again one day. Those stars will have the power to illuminate the immensity of the heavens and no one will ever be able to extinguish them again.

Rome, 1992
Now that Borsellino is dead, no one can understand what emptiness he left in my life.

Everyone is afraid, but as for me the only thing I'm afraid of is that the Mafia State will win and those poor fools battling against windmills will be killed. Before fighting against the Mafia you have to examine your own conscience and then, after you have defeated the Mafia inside yourself, you can fight the Mafia that's in your circle of friends. We ourselves and our mistaken way of behaving are the Mafia.

Borsellino, you died for what you believed in
but without you I am dead.

Final Exam Essay

Assigned Topic: The Problem of the Mafia and Possible Solutions for Eliminating It

In our eyes, the death of any other person would have been expected, we would almost have been impassive before that natural phenomenon, death. But Judge Falcone, for those who have put their faith and hope in him, the hope for a new, clean, honest world, was an example of tremendous courage, an example to follow. With him died the image of a man who fought with lawful weapons against people who attack from behind and stab you in the back, and are proud of it. I wonder for how long people will still talk about his death, perhaps a month, a year, but in all that time only a few of them will have the strength to keep on fighting. Judges, magistrates, collaborators with justice, Mafia *pentiti*[3] who've turned state's witness, are afraid now more than ever, because they feel inside that no one will be able to protect them. If they say too much no one will be able to save them from something they call the Mafia.

But really, they will have to protect themselves only from their friends – members of parliament, lawyers, magistrates, men and women who in the eyes of others have an image of high social prestige and whom no one will ever be able to unmask. We listen, we see, we do what they command. Some do it for money, others out of fear, maybe because your father, commonly speaking, is a boss and you, like him, will be the head of a big organization, the head of men who will do what you want at the snap of a finger. They will serve you, help you make money without considering anything else at all. They have no heart, much less a soul. Their true mother is the Mafia, a way of being that few people understand.

You see, with Falcone's death those men wanted to tell us that they will always win, that they are the strongest, that they have the power to kill anyone. A signal that arrived, stunning and frightening. The initial effects are immediately appearing, the first Mafia *pentiti* will retract their statements. Some of them are afraid, like Contorno, who accuses the justice system of not giving him enough protection. But what can the ministers, police, and carabinieri do? If you ask for protection they provide it, but you realize they do not have the means to ensure your safety, they lack personnel, they lack armoured cars, they lack the laws to ensure no one will discover where you are. They can not give you a new identity. You run away from the Mafia, which has everything it wants, to seek safety in the justice system, which does not have the weapons to fight.

The only hope is to never give in. As long as judges like Falcone, Paolo Borsellino, and so many others like them are alive, we must never give in, and justice and truth will live on in spite of everything and everyone. The only way to eliminate this plague is to make young people who live amidst the Mafia aware that there is another world beyond it, made of simple yet beautiful things, of purity, a world where you are treated for what you are, not because you are the child of so and so, or because you paid the price to have someone do you a favour. Perhaps an honest world will never exist, but who prevents us from dreaming. Perhaps if each one of us tries to change, perhaps we will succeed.
Rita Atria
Erice, 5 June 1992

The Story of My Life

A large mirror in which to look at what you believe you see, where you try to understand but you don't understand. I try to see deeper, but a veil of dark fog prevents you from looking beyond that face, that image full of magic. You attempt to see, but what appears is only a haggard face, two large lips, and two eyes, indescribable, to say the least, bright, but a dark colour, like obscurity, like the night's silence, like two small falling stars. In the image that appears so sweet, melancholy, full of hate, love, disdain, silences that are almost frightening, not one face, but many faces all together, as if nature amused itself by playing and mixing them all up – the mystery that hides behind that image bearing human features. Who knows why such cruel nature wanted to play a trick on that woman, if she really was a woman. I couldn't understand if it was only my imagination that made me see her that way. Her beauty was not easy to glimpse, it was hidden behind who knows what enormous pain, a pain that had worn down her sheathing, the visible, external part. Two eyes that fear made hard and threatening, yet with a mysterious charm, I can't even describe them, after all the time I've spent there looking closely at them. Indescribable also for people who have seen them swollen with tears, tears with the sweetest, lightest taste that lips have ever relished. Who knows why those eyes could not see the sun. Who could ever love her the way she had dreamed of being loved, no one could understand everything she kept inside, everything she had to give, those eyes hid everything, everything she had left by then. Pain, an enormous pain that her heart suffocated inside her, making her become almost cruel in other people's eyes. Not even she could ever have discovered what was hidden in her soul, too complicated. Ever since she was a little girl she had desperately tried to understand what was right and what wasn't. She tried for years and years to discover, to see what everybody had kept hidden from her for so long. But what she discovered hurt her so badly that she could no longer distinguish what was good and what was bad. She had always heard that every person's destiny is marked three days before they are born, and as one is born, so one dies in the end.

Her father was happy to know that the stork, which I believed in as a little girl, would bring him someone to lean on in his old age, as he used to call her. A sweet angel, an intruder in the maternal womb. So much of an intruder that its mother didn't want it, she didn't want another baby to rock, to love, because there had never been any love in that womb. Three months went by and that unwanted baby was put to the test because its mother had decided to get rid of it. So she went to the doctor's office, accompanied by her husband, the father who wanted that baby so much that he went so far as to trick even his wife so that it would be born. First he spoke with the doctor, asking him to diagnose that it would be impossible for his wife to have an abortion, because it could be dangerous for both of their lives. And so that sweet little deceiver of a father was able to have that angel he loved so much brought into the world. Together they endured nine months of suffering and pain, mother and daughter, united for life against great troubles. They waited long days in the hospital because – who knows why – that baby couldn't bring itself to be born. But one day or one night, I don't know which, on the fourth of September, a gorgeous baby girl was born, waited for so long, but loved so little. What happiness her father had in his eyes, that father who loved her with all his heart until his last breath, who tried to give her the best. But there was one thing he could never give her, the love of a real mother, and together with that baby girl he suffered in silence.

She was born by chance, after a son who was ten years old and a daughter who was five, to a father and mother who couldn't love each other. That mother who suffered could do only one thing, pour out her anger on her children. The anger grew inside her because she hadn't been able to build a happy family in her past. What a life for her too. Her mother died when she was just sixteen. Her brother, spendthrift that he was, would even have taken away the air she breathed if he could have, and at the age of twenty-eight, he died in her arms from an awful disease. To see her mother and brother pass away, to have a father who only hurt her, and as years passed he died too. The people she loved had disappointed her, they'd left her alone and with so much pain inside that with time she poured it out on the people close to her. It wasn't her fault, but whose was it then? Who was the author of that cruel destiny? That little girl's first years are a painful memory. She spent the days playing all alone or with her sweet older sister, she didn't have permission to play with the other children, let alone to play outside. Perhaps her mother was over-anxious, we were model children – never play with anything that might get our cute clothes dirty, never sit on the ground, never walk barefoot, never play with other children because they could teach us bad habits, never play with the nicest toys for fear of breaking them. The only thing that wasn't forbidden was the hugs, kisses, loving attentions of papa, that father who, tired from work as he was, found the strength to play with his sweet little girl. Her big brother played with her too, though differently. He would pick her up, toss her flying into the air, and then catch her in his arms, hugging her tightly. He taught her how to dance, and if he had their mother's permission, he used any kind of excuse to take her out of the house. So many times she stumbled, so many times she took the wrong step, so many times she fell, but he was always there to pick her up, to start all over again without ever giving up. He, and he alone there to tell her: Look outside that window that opens onto the world. Life exists, that happy life that maybe we'll have one day too, united together to take turns giving each other strength, or just to hold each other's hand. A dream ... but then who forbade them to dream?

That little girl grew up faster than her years and for the people close to her she had wisdom to spare. But what caused her to be so mature in the way she talked and acted, what was that event that was making her realize little by little what surrounded her? The screams in the night became clear and distinct. Now everything was understandable, that repulsion expressed to her by that maternal voice, which expressed only pleasure, rendered dirty by the surroundings and presence in the midst of which it manifested. Indelible, nearly incomprehensible memories for anyone who hasn't felt the disgust and listened to the strange rustling – and it always comes back to mind – when years later you understand what it really means. Memories that invade your mind, trouble you and leave scars that may perhaps never heal.

The years went by, years of arguing, even about something that wasn't put in the right place, arguing because the children weren't very obedient, or because of the hateful, harsh wife, with anyone, with relatives, friends, in-laws. After the arguments came the blows and the slaps that the husband used to punish his wife for her irritating, entirely unreasonable character. As a consequence, for a week no one at home cooked anymore, no one took care of the three children who fended for themselves. Their mother would stay in bed for a whole week, and when her husband came home in the evening, he prepared something to eat in silence and then, after putting the three children to bed, he went to bed too. It was like a ritual that was perpetuated every day. The older sister – she was only eight – took care of her little sister, doing what she could. Their older brother, Nicola, went to school in the morning and stayed at home in the afternoon amidst the shouting of his mother, who, after duly thrashing him, would shut him up in a room to make him study. He wasn't allowed to play with other children outside either. He had to stay with his mother, helping her now and then to clean, dust, wash the dishes, everything he was able to do since he was a very little boy. And he was in big trouble if he broke anything at all while he was cleaning.

After being beaten with a belt and made to go the entire day without any food, she had to remain standing for about eighteen hours without ever sitting down or leaning on a piece of furniture, she had to stand up straight on her own legs. Anna instead, her older sister, just because she couldn't understand the right order for dividing some math problems made one of her biggest mistakes, which was to ask her mother to explain to her what she had to do. She immediately accused her of not paying attention in school, of having her head up in the clouds, and as punishment she made her get down on her knees in the bathroom in front of the toilet, and she stayed on her knees the rest of the day. This was just one of so many punishments that were inflicted on her. For example, if she broke something, or didn't finish her homework assignments because she didn't know how to do them, she couldn't do anything else except stay the entire night standing on her own two legs without saying a word. Her mother kept an eye on her, sitting on the bed, also because she had slept the day before. They were regularly beaten in turns for the slightest reason, with wooden spoons, belts, or shoes with really hard heels, and then came the various punishments. Someone could say this is horrifying. Instead, it is just something inhuman.

Notes

1 Annina is the mother of Piera Aiello, Rita Atria's sister-in-law.
2 Vincenzo Culicchia was the former mayor of Partanna for over twenty years. Rita Atria alleged that, according to her father, Culicchia had asked the Accardo clan to kill Stefano Nastasi. The Court of Marsala dismissed these charges, but Culicchia was charged with the crime of association with the Mafia.
3 *Pentiti* is a term that goes back to the 1970s in Italy, used first to indicate people on trial for terrorist activities who in the course of the legal proceedings declared themselves *pentiti* (literally repented), and divulged what they knew. The term has been extended to indicate former Italian mafiosi who provide testimony as witnesses for the Italian state.

About the Authors

Rita Atria (1974–92) was born and raised in a family that adhered to Mafia beliefs and codes of behaviour, headed by Vito Atria, a member of the rural Mafia in Partanna. After the deaths of her father in 1985 and then her brother Nicola in 1991, both brutally murdered during Mafia clan warfare, Rita Atria followed the example of her sister-in-law, Piera Aiello, and became a collaborator with justice in early November 1991. Soon transferred to Rome in the witness protection program owing to threats on her life, she worked with Judges Alessandra Camassa and Paolo Borsellino, providing testimony that was crucial to the successful prosecution of numerous mafiosi. In the wake of the horrific Mafia attacks on prominent antimafia figures, which took the lives of Judges Giovanni Falcone (23 May 1992) and Paolo Borsellino (19 July 1992), Rita Atria jumped to her death from the seventh-floor balcony of her safe-house in Rome. Since then, she has become an inspirational symbol of the antimafia struggle and the commitment to justice. Her writings include diary entries, an autobiography she had begun to compose, an exam essay, and her legal testimony as state's witness. Among the numerous works Rita Atria's life has inspired are Sandra Rizza's biography *Una ragazza contro la mafia: Rita Atria, morte per solitudine* (1993, One girl against the mafia: Rita Atria, death from loneliness) and Marco Amenta's award-winning documentary film *Diario di una siciliana ribelle* (1997, English version, *One Girl against the Mafia*).

Letizia Battaglia (1935–) has earned international acclaim for her award-winning works in photography, which have richly documented the dynamic facets of daily living in Sicily, and most particularly

Palermo. She began working as a journalist for the Palermo newspaper *L'Ora* in 1974, shortly before an unprecedentedly horrific Mafia war broke out. In fact, from the late 1970s through 1992, Cosa Nostra murdered countless prominent figures such as police officers, judges, and politicians, as well as some one thousand other victims including mafiosi who were rivals of the Corleone clan and innocent bystanders. The photographic reportage produced by Battaglia forced readers to confront the atrociousness of the Mafia and its effects on society, as illustrated by some of the works published in her book *Letizia Battaglia: Passion, Justice, Freedom* (1999). However, combining remarkable talents with what she calls an intuitive impulse, Battaglia's visual images also offer a particular cultural history of otherwise unimaginable pains of poverty, joys of abandon and neighbourhood celebrations, funerals, and common people engaged in daily occupations as they live the city streets. Indefatigable in her efforts to reclaim the city from Mafia control and deterioration, she has undertaken a variety of enterprises. In 1980 she helped found the Giuseppe Impastato Centre of Documentation; in 1985 she was elected as a member of the Municipal Council of Palermo; from 2000 to 2003 she served as editor of the publication *Mezzocielo*. She currently devotes her time to such projects as the publishing house she founded, which is dedicated to human rights, a women's theatre, and counselling Sicilian prisoners. Among the awards that Battaglia has received are the 1985 Eugene Smith award and the 1999 Mother Johnson Achievement for Life. She is also the subject of Daniela Zanzotto's documentary film *Battaglia*.

Amelia Crisantino (1956–) is among the foremost scholars researching the Mafia in Sicily, having written several important studies that examine it from a historical, social, and cultural perspective. *La mafia come metodo e come sistema* (1989, The Mafia as method and system), co-authored with Giovanni La Fiura, and *Capire la mafia* (1994, Understanding the Mafia) scrutinize the tactics, practices, beliefs, and system of power relations elaborated by the Mafia in the socio-economic and political spheres in the years before the Unification through the 1980s. Her impeccably researched, insightful *Della segreta e operosa associazione: Una setta all'origine della mafia* (2000, About the secret, active association: A sect at the origins of the Mafia) makes use of original archival materials and court documents from the 1870s in an examination of the Stuppagghieri criminal sect that then operated in Monreale and exhibited features that later come to define the Mafia. Focusing on

Palermo as a geographic urban site and lived space are three remarkably diverse books that conjure and explore the rich dimensions of the city. In *La città spugna: Palermo nella ricerca sociologica* (1990, The city-sponge: Palermo in sociological research) Crisantino performs critical readings of sociological theories and interpretations of Palermo, while in her award-winning novel *Cercando Palermo* (1990, Searching for Palermo) evocative perspectives and experiences of a postmodern Palermo dramatize the collision of 'rational' and inexplicable forces. Last, she charts the diasporic spaces fashioned in Palermo, through the testimonies of immigrant women, collected in *Ho trovato l'occidente: Storie di donne immigrate a Palermo* (1992, I've found the west: Stories of women immigrants in Palermo).

Grazia Deledda (1871–1936) launched her long, exceptionally prolific, and talented literary career in 1888 with the short story 'Sangue sardo' (Sardinian blood). Demonstrating tremendous breadth, her works encompass ethnographic writings on Sardinia, her birthplace, critical essays, poetry, plays, novels, and some 250 short stories. Much of the short fiction she wrote from 1912 to 1936 was first published on the cultural page of the *Corriere della sera* newspaper, which showcased stories by Italy's most talented authors, and later appeared in collections. Her varied portraits of bandits, peasants, priests, shopkeepers, the destitute, and the rich tend to explore tragic conflicts that arise as the characters' thoughts, desires, and deeds transgress laws of gender, class, family, or community. In the process Deledda poses fascinating questions about social institutions, justice, inequality, guilt, and power. Several of Deledda's novels attracted international acclaim, earning her the Nobel Prize for literature in 1926. Among these are *Dopo il divorzio* (1902, trans. *After the Divorce*), *Elias Portolu* (1903, Elias Portolu), *Cenere* (1904, Ashes), *Canne al vento* (1913, Reeds in the wind), *Marianna Sirca* (1915, trans. *Marianna Sirca*), and *La madre* (1920, trans. *The Mother*). Also noteworthy is Deledda's autobiography, titled *Cosima, quasi Grazia* (1936, trans. *Cosima*).

Livia De Stefani (1913–91) published her first novel, *La vigna di uve nere* (trans. *Black Grapes*) in 1953, attracting a flurry of responses from fellow authors, critics, and readers. Her vividly drawn depictions of settings in the town of Cinisi and the countryside, and subtle representations of the characters' thoughts, gestures, and psyches as products of the land and society of Sicily prompted several critics to link her work with that of Giovanni Verga and Luigi Capuana. As the plot of murder, passion, incest, and suicide tragically unfolds in the family, headed by the violent mafioso Casimiro Badalamenti, who wields cruel authoritarian power over its members, De Stefani invests the tale with a mythic strain, which elicited hostile responses from both Elio Vittorini and Leonardo Sciascia. Nonetheless, this novel and subsequent works of fiction garnered recognition, particularly for De Stefani's notable abilities to scrutinize diverse social classes and to highlight the equivocal features of their beliefs, emotions, and psychological states verging on psychosis. Shifting her focus from the peasants to the Sicilian upper classes and aristocracy, in *Gli affatturati* (1955, The bewitched) and *La signora di Cariddi* (1975, The Signora of Cariddi) the author portrays the deep-seated biases shaping their ways of thinking, as well as the anxieties, fears, and insanity to which they fall prey. Among De Stefani's other works are a collection of short fiction titled *Viaggio di una sconosciuta e altri racconti* (1963, An unkown female's trip and other short stories), the novel *La stella di Assenzio* (1985, The star of Assenzio), a book of poetry, *Preludio* (1940, Prelude), and *La mafia alle mie spalle* (1991, The Mafia at my back), the autobiographical account of the Mafia's attempts to control the business affairs on her agricultural estate and, ultimately, to acquire the property.

Felicia Impastato (1915–2004) has come to emblematize both the deep conflicts lived by families divided over adherence to Mafia codes of behaviour and the struggle to defeat them, and the possible transformation of family members from conformity with traditional Mafia ways of thinking and acting to antimafia opposition. Wed to Luigi Impastato, Felicia married into a family with strong ties to the Mafia. Luigi Impastato had served time in forced residence during Fascism. He also had long-standing associations with both Gaetano Badalamenti, the infamous Mafia boss of Cinisi, and Cesare Manzella, Impastato's brother-in-law and a prominent mafioso killed in a car-bomb explosion in 1963. By the 1970s, the full spectrum of criminal activities conducted by the Mafia to control, for example, construction, financial dealings, and politics in Cinisi had come under a relentless public attack, undertaken by Giuseppe Impastato (1948–78), Felicia Impastato's son. An innovative, dynamic antimafia activist, he created the Music and Culture Centre in 1975, founded and directed the Radio Aut radio station, and fought for the rights of peasants, construction workers, and young people struggling against the Mafia control of

Cinisi, or *Mafiopoli*, as he dubbed it. On the night of 8 May 1978, a year after his father died in a car crash, Giuseppe Impastato was murdered, blown up on a section of train tracks. As dictated by traditional Mafia practice, the role of Felicia Impastato as mother would have been to observe *omertà*, to keep silent. Instead, she too spoke out publicly against the Mafia and provided information to state prosecutors. In 2001 Vito Palazzolo was found guilty of the murder of Giuseppe Impastato, and in 2002 Gaetano Badalamenti, who ordered the murder, received a life sentence. The oral interview given by Felicia Impastato to Anna Puglisi and Umberto Santino, published as *La mafia in casa mia* (1987, The Mafia in my home), records her invaluable insights about these events and the changes in ideas, values, and actions they inspired. Marco Tullio Giordana's film *I cento passi* (2000, The one hundred steps) narrates the dramatic story, focusing on Giuseppe Impastato's life.

Carolina Invernizio (1851–1916) debuted on the Italian literary scene in 1876 with *Un autore drammatico* (A dramatic author), the first of some one hundred and thirty novels that earned her explosive success among the mass popular audience she cultivated. Her works, many of which were published in instalments in the newspaper *La Gazzetta di Torino*, display richly descriptive elements typical of French authors of the 1800s, as well as the gothic and historical novel. Invernizio created an unforgettable retinue of fascinating female protagonists, male villains, and heroes, embroiled in macabre events, crimes, secrets, nightmares, and fantasies, as suggested by a few of her most famous titles: *Il bacio di una morta* (1886, The kiss of a dead woman), *La vendetta di una pazza* (1894, A crazy woman's vendetta), and *La sepolta viva* (1896, The woman buried alive). Perceiving such stories as a scandalous threat, the Vatican placed works of her fiction on its list of banned books.

Silvana La Spina has lived most of her life in Catania, where she teaches Italian literature and contributes to several newspapers. She has distinguished herself as an award-winning novelist and short-story writer. In *Morte a Palermo* (1987, Death in Palermo), the first of some seven novels and a provocative contribution to the philosophical crime-fiction genre, she elaborates several issues and themes that recur in her fiction. For instance, women's roles in society, popular legends, and classic myths; diverse systems of social power and oppression; notions of crime and justice; and the multiple, conflicting features of Sicily suggested by its landscape, language, history, and culture. Whereas classic myths and diverse models of justice provide clues to the murder of a professor in Palermo in La Spina's debut novel, the historical Separatist Movement, politics, and the Mafia form avenues of inquiry for a young prosecutor seeking justice for the murder of an Honourable Member of Parliament in *L'ultimo treno da Catania* (1992, The last train from Catania). In contrast, the author participates in the literary project of mythic revisionism, creating an innovative rewriting of Penelope from Greek myth in *Penelope* (1998), as the protagonist fashions both her self and a tapestry. As suggested by the title, *La creata Antonia* (2001, The created Antonia) focuses on the formation of women's notions of self. It is the story of a young princess in Catania of the 1700s who, forced to become a nun, teaches her servant Antonia to read and to resist patriarchal norms, as she furnishes her with forbidden books. La Spina's most recent work is in non-fiction, entitled *La mafia spiegata ai miei figli (e anche ai figli degli altri)* (2006, The Mafia as explained to my children [and also to other people's children]). While underscoring the Mafia as a product constructed by men, and therefore subject to defeat, La Spina provides a historical overview of its formation in relation to the feudal system, political figures and parties, Freemasonry, and antimafia figures such as General Dalla Chiesa and Judge Paolo Borsellino.

Luigi Natoli (1857–1941), who adopted the pseudonym William Galt, was born in Palermo and educated as a teacher. He later moved to Rome, and earned recognition as an accomplished journalist, novelist, and literary scholar. He was a contributor to numerous Italian newspapers and magazines, and published critical works on such topics as Giovanni Meli, Garibaldi, Dante, and the ways literature produced by Sicilian authors related to prominent trends in the broader Italian literary tradition. Among the serialized historical novels he penned throughout his career are *Il vespro siciliano* (The Sicilian vesper), *Avventure di un carbonaro* (The adventures of a carbonaro), and *La vecchia dell'-aceto* (The old vinegar woman). Natoli wrote *I Beati Paoli* (The Blessed Paulists) specifically for the newspaper *Giornale di Sicilia*, where it was published in 239 instalments from 6 May 1909 to 2 January 1910. Since then, the work has gone through several reprints in volume form, and has remained an unrivalled best-seller in Sicily.

Giuseppe Ernesto Nuccio (1874–1933) lived most of his life in Palermo, where he devoted himself to bettering the living conditions of children through his vocation as both teacher and writer. He published numerous essays in pedagogical and literary journals on such topics as Italian children's literature, the relations between poverty and juvenile crime, and strategies for educating the masses. Among his works of fiction are short stories, novels, and an impressive array of literature for children and adolescents. Such tales as *Il figlio del brigante* (1911, The brigand's son), *Travolto nel gorgo* (1920, Swept into the whirlpool), and the stories in *Racconti della Conca d'Oro* (1911, Stories of the Conca d'Oro) exemplify how Nuccio fashions his fiction as a form of social and cultural critique. He focuses attention on the forms and effects of extreme poverty, crime, and violence on the day-to-day existence of the lower classes, and children in particular. Indeed, his sometimes gritty, hopeless descriptions of the material conditions confronted by countless children left to fend for themselves on city streets or in the countryside drew objections from some critics of the time.

Maria Occhipinti (1921–96) fashioned a distinct voice in Italian society and culture, presenting new ways of understanding the struggles, customs, ideals, and political values of peasant and working-class communities in Sicily during Fascism and the postwar period. Self-taught and an exceptionally committed activist of the left, she was a protagonist in the *non si parte* ('we won't leave') revolt in Ragusa, her birthplace. On 4 January 1945, as the Italian government made house-to-house searches in poor neighbourhoods in Ragusa, rounding up boys and young men to send to the front, Occhipinti, then five months pregnant, lay down on the street in front of a truck, and the young males escaped. In her autobiography *Una donna di Ragusa* (1957, A woman from Ragusa), Occhipinti provides a singular account of this event and its aftermath, including the sentences of forced residence in Ustica and then prison in Palermo, which she served until her amnesty in December 1946. Particularly insightful are her descriptions of the women, students, and peasants who, depleted by dire living conditions during the war and the 'liberation' of Sicily, took part in the popular revolt against forced conscription, mistaken for decades as a pro-Fascist uprising. Occhipinti's works of short fiction appear in the collection *Il carrubo e altri racconti* (1993, The carob tree and other stories). Portions of her autobiography have been translated into English, and appear in Martha King's *New Italian Women: A Collection of Short Fiction*.

Anna Maria Ortese (1914–96) is the author of numerous award-winning novels and of reportage on her travels through Italy, Russia, England, and France, for instance, which she contributed to such publications as *Noi donne* (We women), *L'Unità* (Unity), and *L'Europeo* (The European). They now appear in the collection *La lente scura: Scritti di viaggio* (1991, The dark lens: Travel writings). Ortese began her literary career in the 1930s, writing short stories, including the collection *Angelici dolori* (Angelic pains). In such works as *Il mare non bagna Napli* (1953, trans. *The Sea is not Naples*), *L'iguana* (1965, trans. *The Iguana*), and *La luna sul muro* (1968, The moon on the wall), Ortese represents thoughts, perceptions, and images in her particular magical-realist manner, as the magical forms a palpable presence in the realities of living. Among recurrent themes elaborated by Ortese are alienation, loss, poverty and misery in the Italian south, exploitation, suffering, and the need for human solace and pity.

Maria Saladino has devoted her life's work to saving the lives of children by giving them shelter, care, education, job training, and employment opportunities. For these purposes, she has founded several youth centres. Drawing upon her experiences, she published the non-fiction collection *Bimbi senza sorriso: dieci storie vere della Valle del Belice* (1991, Children without a smile: Ten true stories of the Belice Valley).

Giovanni Verga (1840–1922) stands among Italy's most extraordinary storytellers for the significance of both the tales he told about Sicily, his birthplace, and his way of telling them. In the mid-1870s, amidst growing evidence of the Italian state's failures to better the dire living conditions of, and socio-economic injustices confronting, the majority of southern Italians, Verga trained his eye on Sicilian peasants and townspeople. Aspiring to craft such a strong illusion of reality that it would appear as if the characters had come spontaneously into being to tell their life stories in their own words, the author depicts particular thoughts, beliefs, codes of behaviour, desires, and fears as inseparable from the Sicilian landscape that gave rise to them. These features distinguish such works as the novels *I Malavoglia* (1881) and *Mastro Don Gesualdo* (1888) (respectively translated into English as *The House by the Medlar Tree* and *Mastro-Don Gesualdo*), the short stories collected in *Vita dei campi* (1880, Life in the fields) and *Novelle rusticane* (1883, Rustic tales), as well as 'The Gold Key,' first published in 1884.

Selected Bibliography

Literature

Azoti, Antonina. *Ad alta voce: Il riscatto della memoria in terra di mafia*. Naples: Terre di mezzo, 2005.

Badalamenti, Gabriella. *Come l'oleandro*. Palermo: Sellerio, 2002.

Balestrini, Nanni. *Sandokan: Storia di camorra*. Turin: Einaudi, 2004.

Bonanni, Patrizia. *La toga bruciata*. Rome: Serarcangeli, 1997.

Bufalino, Gesualdo. *Tommaso e il fotografo cieco*. Milan: Bompiani, 1996.

– *Tommaso and the Blind Photographer*. Trans. Patrick Creagh. London: Harvill, 2000.

Buttafuoco, Pietrangelo. *Le uova del drago*. Milan: Mondadori, 2005.

Buttitta, Ignazio. 'Cantata contru la mafia.' In *Pietre nere*. Milan: Feltrinelli, 1983.

Camilleri, Andrea. *The Shape of Water*. Trans. Stephen Sartarelli. New York: Penguin, 2002.

– *The Terra-cotta Dog*. Trans. Stephen Sartarelli. New York: Penguin, 2002.

– *The Snack Thief*. Trans. Stephen Sartarelli. New York: Penguin, 2003.

– *The Smell of the Night*. Trans. Stephen Sartarelli. New York: Penguin, 2005.

– *Excursion to Tindari*. Trans. Stephen Sartarelli. New York: Penguin, 2005.

Cappellani, Ottavio. *Chi è Lou Sciortino?* Vicenza: Neri Pozza, 2004.

Consolo, Vincenzo. *Lo spasimo di Palermo*. Milan: Mondadori, 1998.

Crisantino, Amelia. *Cercando Palermo*. Palermo: La Luna, 1990.

Cutrufelli, Maria Rosa. *La Briganta*. Palermo: La Luna, 1990.

– *Canto al deserto: Storia di Tina, soldato di mafia*. Milan: Longanesi, 1994.

– *The Woman Outlaw*. Trans. Angela M. Jeannet. New York: Legas, 2004.

Deledda, Grazia. 'Il sicario.' *Corriere della sera*, 22 February 1928, 3.

Denti Di Pirajno, Alberto. *La mafiosa*. Milan: Longanesi, 1965.

De Stefani, Livia. *La vigna di uve nere*. Milan: Mondadori, 1953.

– *Black Grapes*. New York: Criterion, 1958.

– *La mafia alle mie spalle*. Milan: Mondadori, 1991.

Fava, Giuseppe. *Gente di rispetto*. Milan: Bompiani, 1975.

Galasso, Alfredo. *La mafia non esiste*. Naples: Tullio Pironti, 1988.

Guaita, Gianni, and Orietta Guaita. *Isola perduta*. Milan: Rizzoli, 2001.

Invernizio, Carolina. *Le due madri. Un episodio del brigantaggio*. Florence: Salani, 1885.

La Spina, Silvana. *Morte a Palermo*. Milan: La Tartaruga, 1987.

– *Scirocco e altri racconti*. Milan: La Tartaruga, 1992.

– *L'ultimo treno da Catania*. Milan: Bompiani, 1992.

Lentini, Mirella. *Elegia di un assessore pentito*. Pescara: Edizioni Tracce, 1993.

Linares, Vincenzo. *Masnadiere siciliano*. 1841.

Loschiavo, Giuseppe Guido. *Terra amara: La trilogia della siepe*. Rome: C. Colombo, 1956.

Maraini, Dacia. *Bagheria*. Milan: Rizzoli, 1993.

Masciopinto, Rosa. *Donna d'onore*. Palermo: Edizioni della Battaglia, 1996.

Mazzucco, Melania G. *Vita. A Novel*. Trans. Virginia Jewess. New York: Picador, 2006.

Milito, Lynda, and Reg Potterton. *Mafia Wife*. New York: HarperCollins, 2003.

Montemagno, Gabriello. *Il sogno spezzato di Rita Atria*. Palermo: Edizioni della Battaglia, 1992.

Mosca, Gaspare. *La Vicaria di Palermo* (Part 1 of trilogy *Li Mafiusi. Trilogia*). Palermo: V. Giliberti, 1896.

Natoli, Luigi (William Galt). *I Beati Paoli*. In *Giornale di Sicilia*, May 1909–January 1910.

– *I Beati Paoli*. 2 vols. Palermo: S.f. Flaccovio, 1996.

Nuccio, Giuseppe Ernesto. 'Testagrossa acconsente.' In *Racconti della Conca d'Oro*. Florence: Bemporad, 1911.

Occhipinti, Maria. *Il carrubo e altri racconti*. Palermo: Sellerio, 1993.

Ortese, Anna Maria. 'Montelepre.' In *La lente scura: Scritti di viaggio*. Ed. Luca Clerici. Milan: Adelphi, 2004.

Puzo, Mario. *The Godfather*. New York: Signet, 1969.

Saladino, Giuliana. *Terra di rapina*. Palermo: Sellerio, 2001.

Savarese, Nino. *Storia di un brigante*. Milan: Casa Editrice Ceschina, 1931.

Sciascia, Leonardo. *Il giorno della civetta*. Turin: Einaudi, 1961.

– *A ciascuno il suo*. Turin: Einaudi, 1966.

– *To Each His Own*. Trans. Adrienne Foulke. New York: New York Review Books, 2000.

– *The Day of the Owl*. Trans. Archibald Colquhoun and Arthur Oliver. New York: New York Review Books, 2003.

Tomasi Di Lampedusa, Giuseppe. *Il Gattopardo*. Milan: Feltrinelli, 1958.
– *The Leopard*. Trans. Archibald Colquhoun. New York: Pantheon, 1960.
– 'Il mattino di un mezzadro.' In *I racconti*. Milan: Feltrinelli, 1976.
Vassalli, Sebastiano. *Il cigno*. Turin: Einaudi, 1993.
– *The Swan*. Trans. Emma Rose. London: Harvill Press, 1997.
Verga, Giovanni. 'La chiave d'oro.' In *Drammi intimi*. Rome: Sommaruga, 1884.
Violante, Luciano. *Cantata per la festa dei bambini morti di mafia*. Turin: Bollati Boringhieri, 1994.

Selected Film Chronology

In nome della legge. Pietro Germi. 1949.
I mafiosi. Roberto Mauri. 1959.
Salvatore Giuliano. Francesco Rosi. 1961.
Mafioso. Alberto Lattuada. 1962.
L'uomo da bruciare. Paolo and Vittorio Taviani. 1962.
Seduced and Abandoned. Pietro Germi. 1964.
A ciascuno il suo. Elio Petri. 1967.
Il giorno della civetta. Damiano Damiani. 1968.
Il caso Mattei. Francesco Rosi. 1972.
Mimì metallurgico ferito nell'onore. Lina Wertmüller. 1972.
Lucky Luciano. Francesco Rosi. 1973.
The Godfather Part II. Francis Ford Coppola. 1974.
Gente di rispetto. Luigi Zampa. 1975.
Cadaveri eccellenti. Francesco Rosi. 1976.
Cento giorni a Palermo. Giuseppe Ferrara. 1984.
Il pentito. Pasquale Squitieri. 1985.
Dimenticare Palermo. Francesco Rosi. 1990.
Johnny Stecchino. Roberto Benigni. 1991.
La scorta. Ricky Tognazzi. 1993.
Giovanni Falcone. Giuseppe Ferrara. 1993.
Il lungo silenzio. Margarette Von Trotta. 1993.
Palermo-Milano sola andata. Claudio Fragasso. 1995.
Testimone a rischio. Pasquale Pozzessere. 1997.
Tano da morire. Roberta Torre. 1997.
Diario di una siciliana ribelle. Marco Amenta. 1997.
I cento passi. Marco Tullio Giordana. 2000.
Placido Rizzotto. Pasqaule Scimeca. 2000.
I giudici. Ricky Tognazzi. 2000.

Angela. Roberta Torre. 2003.
Segreti di stato. Paola Baroni. 2003.
Il fantasma di Corleone. Marco Amenta. 2004.
Alla luce del sole. Roberto Faenza. 2005.

History and Criticism

Abbate, Lirio, and Peter Gomez. *I complici*. Rome: Fazi Editore, 2007.
Albano, Vittorio. *La mafia nel cinema siciliano da In nome della legge a Placido Rizzotto*. Manduria: Barbieri Editore, 2003.
Arlacchi, Pino. *Men of Dishonor: Inside the Sicilian Mafia*. New York: William Morrow, 1993.
Bartolotta Impastato, Felicia. *La mafia in casa mia: Intervista di Anna Puglisi and Umberto Santino*. Palermo: La Luna, 1987.
Bondanella, Peter. *Hollywood Italians: Dagos, Palookas, Romeos, Wise Guys, and Sopranos*. New York: Continuum, 2004.
Brancati, Elena, and Carlo Muscetta, eds. *La letteratura sulla mafia*. Rome: Bonacci, 1988.
Burnett, Stanton H., and Luca Mantovani. *The Italian Guillotine: Operation Clean Hands and the Overthrow of Italy's First Republic*. New York: Rowman and Littlefield, 1998.
Catanzaro, Raimondo. *Il delitto come impresa: Storia sociale della mafia*. Padua: Livinia Editrice, 1988.
– *Men of Respect: A Social History of the Sicilian Mafia*. New York: Free Press, 1992.
Crisantino, Amelia, and Giovanni La Fiura. *La mafia come metodo e come sistema*. Cosenza: Pellegrini, 1989.
– *Della segreta e operosa associazione: Una setta all'origine della mafia*. Palermo: Sellerio, 2000.
De Stefano, George. 'Ungood Fellas.' *The Nation*, 7 February 2000, 31–3.
Dickie, John. 'Stereotypes of the Italian South 1860–1900.' In *The New History of the Italian South: The Mezzogiorno Revisited*, ed. Robert Lumley and Jonathan Morris, 114–47. Devon, UK: University of Exeter Press, 1997.
– *Cosa Nostra: A History of the Sicilian Mafia*. New York: Palgrave MacMillan, 2004.
Duggan, Christopher. *Fascism and the Mafia*. New Haven: Yale University Press, 1989.
Falcone, Giovanni. *Cose di Cosa Nostra*. Milan: Rizzoli, 1991.
Fazio, Ida. 'The Family, Honour and Gender in Sicily: Models and New Research.' *Modern Italy* 9.2 (November 2004): 263–80.

Fentress, James. *Rebels and Mafiosi: Death in a Sicilian Landscape*. Ithaca: Cornell University Press, 2000.

Fiume, Giovanna. 'Bandits, Violence and the Organization of Power in Sicily in the Early Nineteenth Century.' In *Society and Politics in the Age of the Risorgimento: Essays in Honor of Denis Mack Smith*, ed. J.A. Davis and Paul Ginsborg, 70–91. Cambridge: Cambridge University Press, 1991.

Franchetti, Leopoldo. *Condizioni politiche e amministrative della Sicilia*. Rome: Donzelli, 1993.

Gambetta, Diego. *The Sicilian Mafia: The Business of Protection*. Cambridge: Harvard University Press, 1993.

Jamieson, Alison. *The Antimafia: Italy's Fight against Organized Crime*. London: MacMillan, 2000.

La Spina, Silvana. *La mafia spiegata ai miei figli (e anche ai figli degli altri)*. Milan: Bompiani, 2006.

Levi, Carlo. *Le parole sono pietre*. Turin: Einaudi, 1955.

Lo Bianco, Giuseppe, and Sandra Rizza. *Il gioco grande: Ipotesi su Provenzano*. Rome: Riuniti, 2006.

– *Rita Borsellino: La sfida siciliana*. Rome, Riuniti, 2006.

– *L'agenda rossa di Paolo Borsellino*. Milan: Chiarelettere, 2007.

Lo Verso, Girolamo, ed. *La mafia dentro: Psicologia e psicopatologia di un fondamentalismo*. Milan: FrancoAngeli, 1998.

Lupo, Salvatore. *Storia della mafia*. Rome: Donzelli, 1993.

– 'The Allies and the Mafia.' *Journal of Modern Italian Studies* 2.1 (Spring 1997): 21–33.

Madeo, Liliana. *Donne di mafia: Vittime, complici e protagoniste*. Milan: Baldoni & Castoldi, 1997.

Messenger, Chris. *The Godfather and American Culture: How the Corleones Became 'Our Gang.'* Albany: State University of New York Press, 2002.

Moe, Nelson. *The View from Vesuvius: Italian Culture and the Southern Question*. Berkeley: University of California Press, 2002.

The New York Times on the Sopranos. New York: Pocket Books, 2000.

Occhiogrosso, Franco, ed. *Ragazzi della mafia: Storie di criminalità e contesti minorili, voci dal carcere, le reazioni e i sentimenti, i ruoli e le proposte*. Milan: FrancoAngeli, 1993.

Onofri, Massimo. *Tutti a cena da don Mariano: Letteratura e mafia nella Sicilia della nuova Italia*. Milan: Bompiani, 1995.

Orlando, Leoluca. *Fighting the Mafia and Renewing Sicilian Culture*. San Francisco: Encounter Books, 2001.

Parker, John. *The Walking Dead: A Woman's Brave Stand against the Mafia*. London: Simon & Schuster, 1995.

Paternostro, Dino. *L'antimafia sconosciuta: Corleone 1893–1993*. Palermo: La Zisa, 1994.

Petrignani, Sandra. *Le signore della scrittura: Interviste*. Milan: La Tartaruga, 1984.

Pilati, Giacomo. *Le siciliane: Quindici storie vere*. Trapani: Coppola Editore, 1998.

Pogliaghi, Luigi, ed. *Giustizia come ossessione: Forme della giustizia nella pagina di Leonardo Sciascia*. Milan: La vita felice, 2005.

Rizza, Sandra. *Una ragazza contro la mafia: Rita Atria, morte per solitudine*. Palermo: La Luna, 1993.

Robb, Peter. *Midnight in Sicily*. New York: Vintage, 1999.

Santino, Umberto. 'L'omicidio mafioso.' In *La violenza programmata: Omicidi e guerre di mafia dagli anni '60 ad oggi*, ed. Giorgio Chinnici and Umberto Santino. Milan: F. Angeli, 1989.

– *Storia del movimento antimafia*. Rome: Riuniti, 2000.

Savagnone, Giuseppe. *La Chiesa di fronte alla mafia*. Milan: San Paolo, 1995.

Saviano, Roberto. *Gomorra*. Milan: Mondadori, 2006.

Schneider, Jane, ed. *Italy's 'Southern Question': Orientalism in One Country*. Oxford: Berg, 1998.

Schneider, Jane C., and Peter T. Schneider. 'Mafia, Antimafia, and the Question of Sicilian Culture.' *Politics and Society* 22.2 (June 1994).

– *Reversible Destiny: Mafia, Antimafia, and the Struggle for Palermo*. Berkeley: University of California Press, 2003.

Sciascia, Leonardo. 'Mafia e letteratura.' In *Cruciverba*. Turin: Einaudi, 1983.

Servadio, Gaia. *Mafioso, a History of the Mafia from Its Origins to the Present Day*. London: Secker and Warburg, 1976.

Siebert, Renate. *Secrets of Life and Death: Women and the Mafia*. Trans. Liz Heron. London: Verso, 1996.

– *Storia di Elisabetta: Il coraggio di una donna sindaco in Calabria*. Milan: Pratiche Editrice, 2001.

Stille, Alexander. *Excellent Cadavers: The Mafia and the Death of the First Italian Republic*. New York: Vintage, 1996.

Villari, Pasquale. *Le lettere meridionali ed altri scritti sulla questione sociale in Italia*. 2nd ed. Turin: Fratelli Bocca, 1885.

– *I mali dell'Italia: Scritti su mafia, camorra e brigantaggio*. Florence: Valecchi, 1995.